PASS ME YOUR SHOES

A Couple with Dwarfism

Navigates Life's Detours with Love and Faith

Pass Me Your Shoes is an honest and well-documented memoir that reveals the challenges and successes of the author as a little person. Suffused with loving and humorous anecdotes of family and friends, it is also a testament of faith. Readers will marvel at the grit and tenacity of this author to succeed in life and love. This book provides a thoughtful contribution to the literature of dwarfism.

~ **Carol Wintercorn, Retired Librarian**

Everyone should read *Pass Me Your Shoes*. Angela and Robert Van Etten are two people who have genuinely taken lemons and made lemonade! I have sampled their beverage and it is deliciously bracing. They serve it up with grace and good humor. I know of no one who has faced greater barriers and overcome them with more success than these two. The range of their experiences and quality of accomplishments should be an inspiration to anyone. 'I can't' is not in their vocabulary. Not only did they face down their own unique challenges, but each became an effective advocate for others with similar barriers to full access to opportunities to excel. I pray that their story is widely circulated and anyone who is daunted by a tough circumstance will find inspiration to pursue their dream. Clearly God has blessed their dependence on Him and shown His power to bring them a life filled with rich experiences and deep friendships.

~ **Lee Fielder, former Pastor of Tropical Farms Baptist Church, Stuart, Florida**

Pass Me Your Shoes does indeed allow the reader to walk along with the author on her odyssey through life. With great frankness, Angela relates the challenges and triumphs she has faced in marriage, family, health and career. Along the way, we learn profound lessons from her great humor, strong faith and abiding love.

~ **Diane Tomasik, Retired Journalist and Communications Professional**

What an honor it is to recommend Angela Van Etten's book, *Pass Me Your Shoes.* I love reading biographies and autobiographies. Since I have the privilege of knowing Angela and Robert personally, it is a special treat to read this story of their relationship with each other and with God. It is pure joy to see how God matured them along life's journey and maneuvered them through struggles both big and small.

~ **Darrell Pace, Pastor of Calvary Baptist Church, Tuscumbia, Alabama**

I've known Angela and Robert Van Etten for many years, so I was pleased that she opened the second volume of her autobiography with the story of their meeting, romance, courtship and marriage. She continues with the growth and development of their marriage, professional careers and faith in God. She writes with a delightful sense of humor and does not hesitate to reveal her deep faith in her Lord Jesus Christ.

~ **Dianne Callender, Retired Librarian,**
Tropical Farms Baptist Church, Stuart, Florida

PASS ME YOUR SHOES

A Couple with Dwarfism

Navigates Life's Detours with Love and Faith

Angela Muir Van Etten

Publisher: B New Creations
www.bettyshoopman.com

Printed in the United States of America
1 2 3 4 5 10 9 8 7 6

To the LORD my God
My strength, my rock, my fortress,
my deliverer, my shield, my refuge, my support and my salvation.
You cleared the ground under me so my footing was firm.
∞ Psalm 18:36 MSG

To Robert
My husband of 39 years who has kept his marriage vow
to stand with me no matter what happens and
respect my individuality.

Table of Contents

Table of Abbreviations

AA	The New Zealand Automobile Association
ABA	American Bar Association
Access Board	Architectural and Transportation Barriers Compliance Board
ADA	Americans with Disabilities Act of 1990
ASL	American Sign Language
AVR	Aortic Valve Replacement
CCS	CCS Disability Action
CILO	Coalition for Independent Living Options, Inc.
CLA	Christian Law Association
DC	District of Columbia
EMT	Emergency Medical Technician
ICU	Intensive Care Unit
INR	International Normalized Ratio
JD	Juris Doctorate
LCP	Lawyers Cooperative Publishing
LP	Little Person/People
LPA	Little People of America
LPNZ	Little People of New Zealand
NAD	National Association of the Deaf
NZ	New Zealand
RESNA	Rehabilitation Engineering Society of North America
SBA	Small Business Administration
SCOTUS	Supreme Court of the United States
SED	Spondyloepiphyseal dysplasia
TFBC	Tropical Farms Baptist Church
UPI	United Press International
US	United States
USTA	United States Tennis Association
Y2K	Year 2000

Preface

Dwarfs Don't Live in Doll Houses was published in 1988 by my husband's business, Adaptive Living. This book was a memoir of my early years mixed in with a discussion of issues affecting little people from the point of view of a single person. Because the book was published several years after I married Robert, many people expected to read about the international whirlwind romance of the president of Little People of New Zealand (LPNZ) and the president of Little People of America (LPA).

My typical response was, "Wait for book two." Obviously, it has been a long wait!

Finally, in 2012, a draft manuscript of book two was complete—a 25-year chronicle of our romance and marriage. While life and heart surgery happened, book two was untouched until I retired in 2018. ***PASS ME YOUR SHOES: A Couple with Dwarfism Navigates Life's Detours with Love and Faith*** was updated, revised and finished in 2019—or so I thought.

After beta reader input, I realized the book was too long and appealed to two different audiences. Some readers would be interested in our personal story and others would be more tuned in to our advocacy agenda. As a result, I separated the advocacy material into book three: ***ALWAYS AN ADVOCATE: A Couple with Dwarfism Fight for Independence and Respect.***

Naturally, I would be delighted if people read all three books in the trilogy, but this isn't required as each book stands alone. Even so, reading all three books will give the reader a thorough understanding of how and why Robert and I believe:

Though if one may be overpowered, two can defend themselves.

A cord of three strands is not quickly broken. ∞ *Ecclesiastes 4:12, NIV*

Like any true story, ours is entwined with many negative experiences and can only be told by including some cringe-worthy personal moments. To leave out the ugly wouldn't be fair or accurate. To avoid damaging the reputations of others, I use generic descriptions or pseudonyms instead of actual names where necessary. My prayer is that people will learn from our experiences—the mistakes we and others made—so that history does not repeat itself. After all, nothing is impossible with God.

Chapter 1
My Heart Beat Faster

Washington Arrival

I jumped off the bottom step of the Dulles airport bus into a dimly lit Washington, DC, neighborhood. The 12 to 15 inch jump was required because my knees don't bend, and there was no handrail to aid my descent. I made a safe landing onto the sidewalk 8,500 miles from home, but I was exhausted—it was nearly midnight—and no one was there to greet me.

I wasn't surprised. Harriet Stickney had already told me she'd failed in her attempt to get the president of Little People of America (LPA) to meet me at the airport. As LPA's national correspondent, she viewed my position as president of Little People of New Zealand (LPNZ) worthy of a presidential welcome, not to mention extending the courtesy to a female in an unknown territory at night. After all, Harriet and her husband, Al, had shown me legendary hospitality in their San Francisco home for an entire week.

But there was no persuading President Bobby Van Etten. His January move to Arlington, Virginia, from the small town of Jupiter, Florida, hadn't prepared him for driving in DC, so he was more afraid of getting lost than any wrath coming his way from Harriet. Thankfully, a cab was available to transport me safely to my room at the International Guest House.

The guesthouse hosts were impressed that flowers preceded my arrival. When Bobby was unable to persuade Ernie—a friend and lifetime resident of the area—to meet me at the airport, the two greeted me with flowers instead. And a note from Bobby asking me to call him in the morning.

New Zealand Embassy Meeting

We met the next day at the NZ Embassy. The advantage was definitely mine, as Harriet had shared her opinion of the man and a few media articles written about him.

Bobby had moved from Florida in January 1981 for a job as a communications engineer for the Architectural and Transportation

Barriers Compliance Board (Access Board). Unfortunately for Bobby, President Reagan made good on his 1980 campaign promise to shrink the federal government. As his first official act after his inauguration, Reagan ordered a hiring freeze retroactive to January 20, 1981. Bobby had already acted on the written job offer, moved from Florida, signed an apartment lease, and reported to work on January 26, 1981. He was among the 1,800 workers shocked to learn that his position was eliminated. The national media covered Bobby's story as a hardship case:

Little People's President Has Conservative Views Tested

Job Freeze by Reagan is Upheld

Left out in cold, he chips at ice on federal hiring[1]

Bobby's knowledge of me was limited to what Harriet had told him—I was president of LPNZ and a lawyer on a Winston Churchill Fellowship. However, he didn't know that my fellowship brought me to the United States for three months to research disability civil rights laws and public relations programs designed to improve attitudes towards people with disabilities, and he didn't know that LPA was 1 of 40 disability organizations included in my research. His engineering (analytical) mind assumed that a little person with a government fellowship was probably middle-aged with a diagnosis of achondroplasia—the most common type of dwarfism. He imagined me on the plump side at about four feet tall.

On Saint Patrick's Day, 1981, Bobby discovered that his assumptions were all wrong. I was a petite 27-year-old with Larsen Syndrome , a very rare type of dwarfism. When Bobby walked towards my desk in the NZ Embassy library, he was all smiles. For some inexplicable reason my heart beat faster as he got closer to me. I don't remember a thing he said. I was unnerved by the proximity of his brown eyes gazing directly into mine. We were eye-to-eye because we were the same exact height—and that connection rarely happens to a little person.

Our First Outing

The NZ Embassy was a convenient place for Bobby to meet me at the beginning of a planned day of sightseeing. Our first stop was the Lincoln Memorial. It didn't take me long to understand Bobby's concern about getting lost on his way to the airport. In broad daylight, he was quite flustered finding his way to the Memorial. And the more lost he got, the faster he drove. He even resorted to asking me for directions—someone who had been in DC for less than 24 hours and could not even see out the car window.

Bobby eventually found his way; we parked and made our way across the street. He then graciously extended his hand to help me up a curb. However, he didn't release my hand after both my feet were set on the sidewalk. Not ready for such a bold move, I let go of his hand. After all, this could hardly be called a date.

We chose the elevator as a good alternative to the 57 steps to President Lincoln's statue that towered above us at more than six times our height. As presidents of two disability organizations, we couldn't help but be inspired by the display of Lincoln's words from the Gettysburg address: *all men are created equal.* We both knew what it was like to be treated as second-class citizens and shared a life mission to achieve equality for little people and others with disabilities.

Pizza was our choice for the evening meal. Corned beef and cabbage never crossed our minds until a drunken Irishman saw the arrival of two little people as a sign of his good luck. We had forgotten about the holiday. He invited himself to our table to share Irish jokes, an intrusion we tolerated for a few minutes. I was relieved and impressed with Bobby's diplomacy as he took charge when the man asked us to join him at the Saint Patrick's Day parade. Bobby declined the offer and persuaded him to move along. Instead of going to the parade, Bobby returned me to my guesthouse where he was more interested in kissing me good night on the cheek than kissing any blarney stone.

The First Two Weeks

In stark contrast to his initial refusal to meet me at the airport, Bobby wasted no time in making up for it—going way beyond what Harriet ever expected of him. He became the ideal host. Because he was unemployed—thus rarely able to afford eating out—he cooked meals for me and arranged for us to dine in the homes of several LPA friends and family.

On my first weekend in Washington, DC, we visited the Smithsonian National Air and Space Museum, an outing which suited Bobby's budget since admission was free.

Many museum patrons who recognized him from the media asked him, "Have you got your job back yet?"

During the following week, Bobby went beyond tour guide and drove me to many of my fellowship appointments. Before taking me back to the guest house in the evening, we would often share a meal. The more time we spent together, the more we got to know each other. Aside from our height compatibility of three feet four inches, we had many things in common:

- First year or two of life dominated by surgeries, hospitals, and rehabilitation centers
- Orthopedic issues limiting our mobility
- Humble financial beginnings
- Fathers who were both bricklayers and football players
- Several younger siblings—I was the eldest of three children and Bobby the eldest of four brothers with one older sister
- A rich relationship with grandparents, aunts, uncles, and cousins
- Beloved memories of family dogs
- A professional college degree
- The recent death of a parent—Bobby's father in 1979 of colon cancer, and my mother in 1980 of melanoma cancer
- An independent spirit able to persevere through adversity
- A strong, outgoing personality
- A distinctive laugh memorable to those who hear it
- A love of travel
- And, most importantly, a belief in God and salvation through His Son Jesus Christ

After 10 days of reveling in each other's company, I wrote a letter home saying how hard it would be to leave him at the end of my four weeks in DC. Then, without warning, we hit a bump in the road when Bobby created a threesome. He invited me to have pizza with him and his friend, Lorraine, who was visiting from out of state. The evening went well enough, but I did wonder about Bobby's relationship with Lorraine. I reluctantly agreed to join them the next day to visit an art museum. Bobby was to phone me the next morning to set the pickup time.

When Bobby did not call me, I tried calling him but could not get through until almost lunchtime. He said that he and Lorraine would come for me at 1:00 p.m. I was aggravated because I had skipped breakfast in order to get a little extra sleep and no lunch was served at the International Guest House. Besides, I had wasted the entire morning.

I waited outside on the front porch to enjoy the warm sunny day. And I waited and waited and waited. After an hour and a half, Bobby finally called to say he was just leaving his apartment. He and Lorraine eventually showed up at 3:00 p.m. in the afternoon. Not only was I quietly fuming, I was also starving. Brunch at the museum was no longer an option and we barely got there in time for an afternoon snack and a peek at a few pieces of art.

How was I supposed to know that I was tagging along as the third wheel? Lorraine obviously saw it this way, while Bobby's view was a little more ambiguous. He paid attention to both of us. I determined not to let this happen again. If Bobby wanted to spend time with me, he would have to initiate the contact.

As a result, I did not see Bobby the next day. Instead, I enjoyed the Museum of American Art by myself. My day did end with a surprise phone call from Bobby at 10:00 p.m. after I was in bed. He apologized for not calling me earlier and arranged to meet me the next day.

March 30, 1981, should have been a typical day in my fellowship experience. My appointment with the National Association of the Deaf (NAD) began with the usual introductions to staff, but I did not learn too much before chaos ensued. Employees frantically ran into the room where I was meeting and signed in American Sign Language (ASL) to my host. I did not know ASL, but something was terribly wrong. The interpreter told me that President Reagan had been shot outside the Washington Hilton hotel and rushed to the hospital. Thankfully, the assassination attempt failed.

My education on deaf issues continued the next day at the Supreme Court of the United States (SCOTUS). Ordinarily, visitors are only allowed to pass through the courtroom in a moving line; but with a letter from the NZ Ambassador, I was able to sit in the attorney gallery for the whole hour. I heard the oral arguments for a Texas case in which a graduate student who was deaf alleged that the University of Texas had violated § 504 of the Rehabilitation Act of 1973 by refusing to pay for a sign language interpreter. Disability advocates were hopeful that this case would establish precedent for requiring institutions receiving federal funds to pay for accommodations that level the playing field for people with disabilities. When SCOTUS published its decision three months later, it was a big letdown when they sidestepped the issue and remanded the case back to the lower court.

The evening was spent with friends from the University of Auckland, New Zealand. Richard had been in my law school class and was working at the Australian Embassy; his wife, Noeline, was a teacher and working at the NZ Embassy.

This unexpected crossing of paths so far from home led an embassy employee to comment, "What a small world."

In a split second, she looked as if she wanted the floor to swallow her whole and began to profusely apologize. I rescued her by assuring her that small is not a taboo word for little people, and that I was about to make the same observation.

Chapter 2
Whirlwind Romance

Turning Point

More than 40 hours passed before I talked to Bobby again—and, yes, I was counting. He was quite frustrated when I did not return his call right away on March 31st and even more so after we played phone tag most of the next day. When we finally connected, I realized he wanted to share his good news with me. He'd made headlines again:

Long Worthwhile Wait: Job Finally Comes Through for Hardship Case
It's Like Being Rescued from a Sinking Ship
Dwarf Wins Long Battle for Federal Job[1]

I was thrilled he had gotten his job back, but even more excited to know that his inability to reach me made him realize how much he cared for me. We'd reached a turning point in our relationship. Now we acknowledged that something special was happening—yet, we were also very aware of our narrow window of time. My fellowship plans in Washington, DC, ended in only two weeks.

Our desire to make the most of every minute led me to make a very foolish decision. Instead of waiting for God to work out the details of our relationship, I took matters into my own hands. I checked out of the guesthouse and moved into Bobby's apartment. I knew it was wrong. I could not even bring myself to tell the house hosts the specifics of where I was going. Instead, I told them I was moving to stay with an LPA member who lived near the subway. Although this was true, I did not say that this member was Bobby Van Etten or that my interests were more than practical.

From a secular standpoint, the decision made perfect sense. Bobby did live close to a subway station, I wouldn't have to worry about meeting the guest house curfew, and I would get to know Bobby better.

I was there to see Bobby sworn in as a federal employee on April 6th. I was also there when a cousin-in-law's call completely knocked off his socks. She advised him that he should not miss his chance with me. Bobby respected her opinion and her advice got him thinking seriously about our future.

In the next few evenings, we continued the meal circuit with Bobby's LPA friends. On April 11th, the day Ronald Reagan returned to his Presidential duties in the White House, Bobby put on his presidential hat at an LPA parent organization conference in the DC area, giving me a great opportunity to see an LPA activity as part of my fellowship study.

Falling in Love

Although it was the eve of my departure for New York City, this was not our farewell. We had both changed our plans to give us two extended visits in May: once at the District 2 LPA regional in Moorestown, New Jersey, and again in DC for the annual conference of the President's Committee on Employment of People with Disabilities.[2]

But first, we had two weeks apart in April to separately ponder the future of our relationship. Although we weren't ready to make any public announcements, we independently chose the same day to tell our parents that we were in love. Bobby and I talked on the phone almost every night about how much we loved and missed each other. At Easter, I enjoyed reconnecting with two brothers from my home church in New Zealand who now lived in Toronto, Canada, with their Canadian wives. Still, Bobby was never far from my mind as I watched the Love Boat on TV and visited Niagara Falls, one of the most popular honeymoon destinations ever.

When I'd been preparing to leave New Zealand on my three-month fellowship, a client gave me this outlandish advice: "If someone proposes, say yes."

At the time, that notion seemed ridiculous. Now it no longer sounded so far-fetched.

On my train trip from Toronto to New York, I wrote a letter home sharing with my father some thoughts about our relationship:

> *Bobby is in love [but] he worries that his behavior is irrational!*
> *. . . Bobby said we make a good team, both able to take the lead, but neither needing or wanting to dominate the other, we each encourage, respect and love the other. . . . One problem is the impracticability of loving someone on the other side of the world.*

We laid aside our mutual concerns about a long-distance relationship.

Bobby invited me to Florida to meet his family in the middle of May. And we made the most of our time together at the two conferences. My roommate at the District 2 regional was kind enough to invite me to her New Jersey home for a couple of nights. Beth's fiancé lived in Atlanta, Georgia, and she had some excellent tips on how to handle a long-distance relationship.

Engagement

After returning to DC, Bobby and I were both very aware that our time together was running out. On May 8, 1981, Bobby said he loved me and wanted to marry me. While his words definitely had the ring of a proposal, the jewelry box he gave me held a watch—not an engagement ring. Since I knew he could not afford a ring, his gift and the special moment marked his commitment to make marriage happen.

Next came the moment I got a little overwhelmed with the decisions facing us: Would we marry in New Zealand, the United States, or both? How long would we wait for the wedding? In which country would we live and work? Which one of us would move halfway around the world?

After two days of deliberations—not exactly the stuff of romance—the details were worked out and I said yes. We announced our engagement on Mother's Day when we called my father in New Zealand, Bobby's mother in Florida, and his cousin-in-law in Virginia. To our surprise, the lightning speed of our seven-week relationship did not cause any of them to suggest putting on the brakes. The only concern anyone expressed came from Bobby's mother, who asked him what color I was. Perhaps she was picturing me in a grass skirt or remembering Bobby teasing his father about dating women from other countries and races.

For me, it was a bittersweet day as I reflected on Mother's Day only one year earlier when my mother lived her last full day on earth. She died in the early morning hours of May 12, 1980. I knew she would have loved Bobby, but I also knew she would have resisted the idea of me moving to America. I remembered how upset she was when my sister moved to Australia, which was only three hours travel compared to the 24 hours to the US east coast.

Our plan was for me to return to New Zealand to complete my Winston Churchill Fellowship duties. Bobby would come to New Zealand for a December wedding with my family and friends, after which I would immigrate to the US as his wife. A month later, we would have a second marriage ceremony in Florida with Bobby's family and friends. We would then fly north to set up residence in Arlington, Virginia, where Bobby lived.

The idea of two wedding ceremonies came from our observation of other little people with long distance relationships. It was a cost-effective way of including both families in the celebration. The basis for the decision for me to live in America was that Bobby would have a harder time finding NZ work in the specialized field of rehabilitation engineering than I would as a US attorney.

"We have a lot to look forward to," Bobby said when he took me to the airport two days after our engagement.

Knowing that in four days I would detour from my fellowship stops for the Florida rendezvous with Bobby's family and friends tempered my sadness.

As planned prior to our engagement, I accompanied Bobby to his college friend's wedding in Orlando. I appreciated the warmth of his many friends and imagined myself as a bride with my own wedding guests in about six months.

After the wedding, Bobby's brother John met us in Orlando and drove us to Stuart where their mother lived. He spontaneously asked if we wanted to stop off in Disney World on the way. *What?* This was on my bucket list of things to do one day, but dropping in for a couple of hours was unreal. Entrance fees were more affordable back then so we went into the Magic Kingdom for a fast circuit of the main attractions.

My rocket blast off on the Space Mountain roller coaster was insane. John convinced me it was safe for a little person, but on the way into the ride I had grave reservations when I saw the almost vertical image of a space traveler's rocket that I would soon be sitting in. Doubt quickly changed to terror as I sped around the mountain in the dark, making sudden direction changes so severe that I thought my head was going to fall off. I saw stars that weren't Disney decor. My neck, my spine, and my falling-four-inches-short-of-the-height-requirement screamed out that this ride was hazardous to my health.

Thankfully, I lived to tell the story in my visits with Bobby's family and LPA members of the South Florida Mini-Gators chapter. I soon discovered that the only things people knew about New Zealand were trout fishing, kiwis, and rabbits. Bobby's brothers were interested in the trout and it was general consensus among the LPA members that rabbits were an endangered species in New Zealand. This was news to me. It turned out they were reading from a very outdated encyclopedia. Nevertheless, I enjoyed everyone's attempts to make me feel welcome.

It was all too soon before Bobby and I were at the airport saying goodbye again. This was a tough farewell, as we did not expect to see each other again for six months. Bobby returned to his job at the Access Board in DC, and I closed out the last two weeks of my fellowship with meetings in Chicago and Los Angeles.

More than 8,600 Miles Apart

Upon returning to New Zealand, I took a locum job for an attorney taking a leave of absence. However, I soon realized that six months was barely enough time to handle my To-Do List:

- Plan the wedding
- Obtain approval for US permanent residency
- Complete the fellowship obligations of writing my report, public speaking engagements, and media interviews
- Spend time with and say goodbye to family and friends
- Take on a new-albeit-temporary job

Something had to give. Because I was living with my father and had very low overhead, I was able to give up the job. I could not have done that without his help.

Long distance communication with Bobby was very challenging. In 1981, we didn't have Internet, e-mail, Facebook, Twitter, or texting—and fax technology was still not popularized. It was not quite a case of quill and ink, but for the most part our communications were limited to pen and paper and a postal service that took two weeks to deliver each way. The answer to a question asked today would not come for at least four weeks.

Oh, yes—at least we had the telephone. But at $1.50 per minute for international phone calls, we reserved our phone time for wedding and immigration questions that needed an immediate answer. In one of these calls, Bobby asked me if it mattered that his custom-tailored wedding suit was cream instead of white. My response sent him back to the tailor.

Letter writing went well for about three weeks. I wrote a couple of times a week and heard from Bobby at least once a week. Although we both had trouble reading the other's handwriting, we were highly motivated to read and reread until we deciphered the words of love, missing one another, and anticipating being together again. We also discussed my law school options, the engagement announcement in the home newspaper, my ring size, designing the wedding invitation—and the newest opportunity to consider: moving to Baltimore for Bobby's dream job at Johns Hopkins Hospital.

Because writing was tedious for Bobby, he looked for an alternative means of communication. He first suggested we communicate via amateur radio. He even sent me the name of an amateur radio operator who could patch in for me on the radio frequencies Bobby gave me. When Bobby did not hear from me on the radio, he correctly concluded that I had no intention of trekking to a stranger's house to relay such private conversations. Besides he had not considered the challenge of connecting live with someone in a time zone 17 hours ahead.

Not one to give up easily, Bobby came up with another plan, "Let's use micro-cassette tapes."

I was on board with this and liked the idea of hearing his voice. I began sending tapes and letters and looked forward to receiving his tapes and the occasional letter. Instead, I heard nothing from him for five weeks. I did not even hear from him on my birthday. I knew he was busy, but he could not possibly be busier than me.

Despite the breakdown in communication, I was not concerned that he had changed his mind. Rather, I just sent him a card with a clear message:

In sympathy for the loss of your pen.

It worked. Bobby realized his mistake immediately. Those five-minute messages he had been diligently recording for me every night were all on the same tape—which he planned to mail when the tape was full. Can you imagine how long it takes an engineer, i.e., man of few words, to fill a 90-minute tape? After receiving my sympathy card, it took him no time at all to find his pen, send tapes, and even spice things up with the occasional gift.

News of our engagement was published in the September issue of *LPA Today*.

Ed Lang, a little person friend and the editor, headlined an article:

Prince Bob to wed Lady Angela[3]

Ed was inspired by the marriage of two LP presidents as well as the 1981 royal wedding of Prince Charles and Lady Diana. He was also partial to an old British slogan: *The sun will never set on little people.*

Immigration and Wedding Plans

By September, we were both feeling the pressure of time regarding wedding plans. So much to do. The following list captures a few of the details to be addressed:

- Pre-marriage counseling in separate countries
- Buying airline tickets
- Writing a wedding invitation that satisfied the traditional preferences of Bobby's mother
- Choosing a method of contraception
- Ordering wedding rings
- Custom-tailoring a wedding suit and gown

My US immigration presented some unexpected timing issues. I *just happened* to meet the assistant to the Consulate General in Auckland, a branch of the US Embassy in Wellington at a speaking engagement a couple of months before the NZ wedding. Her assistance with the immigration process was critical to my being able to enter the US with Bobby in time for the Florida wedding. God's provision, again.

Ordinarily a permanent-resident visa application based on marriage to a US citizen is not filed until after the marriage date. The process normally takes longer than one month and we had only planned two weeks after the NZ wedding before our departure for the USA. Thankfully, the consulate general's assistant agreed to begin my background check and accept medical exam reports prior to the wedding.

Finally, our time apart was almost over. As Bobby wrote,

> *. . . am counting the days until I can hold you again to look into your eyes and see you smile again . . . I love you with all my heart . . . I think of you often even in my dreams. Can't wait to having you always by my side . . . it won't be long . . . my deepest love.*

Chapter 3
A Cord of Three Strands

Bobby's NZ Arrival

No one had to persuade me to go to the airport to meet the president of LPA on October 14, 1981. Five months of waiting made me more than ready to welcome Bobby into my arms in Auckland, New Zealand. My father and Auntie Nan were almost as excited as I was to see the man they had heard so much about.

And there he was coming towards us with his beaming smile. However, his appearance stunned me—literally taking my breath away when he hugged me. Venturing out on Columbus Day on his first overseas trip, didn't he know that 36 hours traveling required a carry-on bag with toiletries and a change of clothes? He arrived in true Christopher Columbus style: unshaven, unkempt, unwashed, and in the same clothes he wore when he left Florida.

My surprise turned to gratitude when Bobby explained how he almost missed his flight. On his Florida stopover to make final wedding plans, he went scuba diving with his brother John the day before departure. Exhausted from the exertion, he slept through the 4:30 a.m. alarm. He only had 20 minutes to throw everything into his suitcase and race to the airport.

Immigration Marriage Ceremony

Bobby got a surprise of his own when I told him we would be getting married the next day. Our original plan was to be married two weeks later on October 31st. When Bobby realized his bachelorhood was ending in less than 24 hours, he joked that I was making sure he did not change his mind. Rather, the US consulate needed at least four weeks after the marriage to process my permanent resident visa application. For this, they needed a marriage certificate.

There were two options. We could wait to marry in the church wedding as planned on October 31st and Bobby could go to the Florida wedding without his bride; or, we could add a civil ceremony on October 15th so that my visa could be processed in time for me to be at his side in the Florida wedding.

I told him, "It's your choice, and you've got one night to sleep on it."

Bobby chose to officially marry me the day after his arrival. My dad and Auntie Nan witnessed the private ceremony in the minister's office. That afternoon we hand-delivered the marriage certificate to the US consulate office.

It was the clerk's turn to be surprised. She asked, "Why are you in my office and not on your honeymoon?"

Although October 15, 1981, is the date on our marriage certificate, we dubbed it our immigration wedding—a formality. We did not consider ourselves married until the NZ church wedding on October 31st. This was the published date for all our guests, the date of the Christian ceremony, and that of our public celebration.

We still had two weeks to visit friends and family, wrap up church wedding plans, sightsee in Rotorua, and give Bobby a bachelor party. The media responded to a press release about Bobby as the guest speaker of the LPNZ national conference, my Winston Churchill Fellowship, and our international romance.

One reporter noted that Bobby's opening address at the LPNZ conference coincided with United Nations Day. The Wellington Evening Post quoted Bobby's description of our union as "an invincible combination in the campaign to gain rights for people with disabilities."[1]

Inevitably, some reporters could not resist the puns with headlines such as:

A little love has gone a long, long way . . .[2]

We preferred the headline of Amanda Samuel's November 23rd article published in the New Zealand Woman's Weekly:

Just two people in love, beginning a new life . . . like millions before them.

The article also noted the reason we allowed the wedding to be televised for a *Close Up* documentary:

. . . to tell the story of two little people doing what every other young couple in love do—getting married.[3]

It was sad that my mother did not live to plan the church wedding with me. However, the generosity and talent of friends blessed me with my wedding dress, wedding cake, and flowers. Since pizza was my first meal with Bobby, it was fitting that we ate pizza at the rehearsal dinner. Except for the presence of the television film crew, it was almost like any other family event at Janet and Ray's. Because Bobby did not have any family or friends in New Zealand, my family and friends were in the wedding party for both the bride and groom.

Presbyterian Church NZ Marriage Ceremony

Dad waited until the morning of the church wedding to take me aside and say, "Don't forget if it doesn't work out, you can always come home."

He wasn't as concerned with my getting married as he was my leaving everyone and everything behind. But I couldn't wait to exchange marriage vows with the man I loved:

> *We will stand by each other no matter what happens,*
> *respecting each other's individuality,*
> *understanding the other's needs,*
> *accepting our changes,*
> *and enjoying our love until death parts us.*

Reverend Andrew Bell closed the ceremony with this benediction:
> *May God the Father bless you,*
> *May Christ the Son take care of you,*
> *The Holy Spirit enlighten you,*
> *And the Lord be your Defender and Keeper,*
> *Now and always, Amen.*

The media attracted so much attention to the wedding that when we came out of the church as husband and wife a sea of people surrounded us. The Cook Island church members placed shell leis around our necks, and my cousin's daughter Keziah gave us a lace horseshoe. The crowd parted as we walked to the wedding car driven by Uncle Peter. After a photo shoot, we returned for a finger-food reception in the church hall. Uncle Stew was the master of ceremonies and we broke tradition by both giving speeches.

For me, it was a wedding reception and farewell party.

Photo Credit: Richard Wells, staff photographer for the Orlando Sentinel, November 28, 1981
Angela and Bobby's bridal love and lace

Catholic Church Florida Marriage Ceremony

Following through with our immigration ceremony paid off. My permanent resident visa came through in time for the Florida wedding to happen with both a bride and groom. I had no idea what to expect at this third ceremony on November 28, 1981. This is the wedding I attended—Bobby and his sister, Paula, did all the planning.

Although the second and third ceremonies were both in church, the similarities beyond that were few. Our NZ wedding was in the Presbyterian tradition of my childhood, while our Florida ceremony was in the Catholic tradition of Bobby's childhood. Again, friends and family were part of the service, but I experienced some culture shock with the size of the wedding party: three groomsmen, five bridesmaids, a flower girl, a ring bearer, a matron of honor and a best man—14 people counting the bride and groom. NZ bridal parties are typically smaller; there were only six in that church ceremony.

Other concerns cropped up as we put final touches on the Florida ceremony. Several members of the wedding party could not make the rehearsal, including Bobby's brother Peter who had pneumonia and missed the wedding altogether. Part of the rehearsal took place in the parking lot because no one had keys to the church. After budgeting the NZ wedding so carefully, my tears flowed when we had to pay for a band we neither wanted nor could afford.

Before the church service, Bobby spent time alone with Father Mike, a childhood friend and the priest who was the marriage celebrant. Because I was not Catholic, I was excluded from this session and was left in the church foyer with the rest of the wedding party—greeting guests, and fielding questions from about six reporters.

About two minutes before the hour, Bobby returned, announcing that he'd left our wedding vows at the motel. About the same time, Paula noticed that her daughter, Juliette, was wearing tennis shoes instead of her junior bridesmaid shoes. Jimmy went to get the vows, and Paula decided Juliette could wear her tennis shoes—instead of making her go barefoot with tears streaming down her face. Crises averted. We heaved a collective sigh of relief and cued Aunt Rita to begin playing the organ.

Paula and her cousin, Phil, led off the procession, except Paula forgot her bouquet. The petals sprinkled by Jennifer Arnold and Brian Campanella beautifully paved our path to the altar. In keeping with Bobby's Dutch heritage, we walked the aisle together, a fitting tradition since we were already married.

Even with all of the extra stress—both good and bad—we were pleased with the decision to have two church ceremonies. In our thank you card to the church wedding guests, we wrote:

Our dual marriage celebration doubled our blessing and strengthened our commitment to each other.

We lost count of the media articles about our wedding, but we did see local, national and international print coverage. Months later, a neighbor returned from Finland with a magazine article on the wedding. We only understood two words—Angela and Bobby—but the photos confirmed it was our wedding story.

The press conveyed the message we intended—that the concept of dwarfs getting married is nothing extraordinary. Despite the cheesy headline, we liked the content of John Hicks' article:

Two little people take THE BIG STEP

In many ways, the marriage of Angela Muir and Bobby Van Etten was a traditional one, wrapped in white lace, trimmed with flowers, tied by love. That was as it should have been—never mind that the bride and groom are both 3-foot-4-inch dwarfs . . . the pair's union . . . shone with far more symbolism than does the average exchange of vows. It was a reaching toward normalcy. . . . It was a way of saying "I can!" in a world that so often shouts "You can't!" to those who are different.[4]

New Zealand Honeymoon

A tractor-trailer truck steering straight at us almost ended our honeymoon before it began. A quiet country road in the Waipua Forest Sanctuary, northwest of Dargaville should have been a safe place for Bobby to practice driving; however, I didn't anticipate his challenge of driving on a metal (gravel) surface.

I had just finished telling him to drive in the middle tracks of the road carved out by prior traffic—per country-gravel-road rules—when I suddenly yelled, "Pull left! PULL LEFT!"

I hadn't yet explained that when oncoming traffic approaches, both vehicles slow down, and pull out of the center tracks to their left. As the gigantic truck appeared from around the corner and sped toward us in the same center tracks we were in, Bobby held to his position in the center. Somehow amid my yelling and the imminence of a head-on collision, Bobby finally pulled left. The truck flew by leaving a trail of dust and our shattered nerves behind him. God saved us from sudden death, and that was the end of Bobby's driving on NZ country roads.

Bobby willingly returned to the passenger seat to enjoy the scenery of the Kauri Coast and the sub-tropical rainforest. The feather-like ferns that surrounded Tane Mahuta (Lord of the Forest) soon calmed both of us. Bobby was in his element, photographing his bride next to the largest kauri tree in New Zealand. At 1,200 years old, this tree stood tall in the forest at 51.5 meters, with a crown spreading 1,000 square meters. The alternative plight of thousands of kauri before it was to stand aboard ships as masts and spars.

Our destination was the Bay of Islands. As we began our journey of discovering one another as husband and wife, we returned to the beginnings of NZ European history. We visited Oihi, the site of my country's first permanent European settlement, first Christian service for a Maori and European congregation (1814), first European birth, first European cemetery, and first school. Paihia, founded as a missionary station in 1823, combined history with Bobby's love of the sea. From here, we boarded a half-day cruise around many of the 200 islands and actually drove through the famed Hole in the Rock on Motukokako Island.

As a lawyer, the town of Russell appealed to me as the first capital of New Zealand. As a Roman Catholic fisherman's son, the historic port appealed to Bobby as an important whaling center and the 1842 site of the first Roman Catholic Mission to New Zealand—Pompallier Mission House. We were both drawn to Maiki Hill for the history of the flagstaff, the original symbol of British authority. Hone Heke, a local Maori chief, was one of the first signers of the Treaty of Waitangi.[3] He became disenchanted with British rule in 1845, and on three separate occasions expressed his discontent by cutting down the flagstaff flying the British Union Jack.

On our return to Auckland, we were amazed by God's timeless influence in nature. In an unassuming farm location south of Kawakawa, we visited the little known Waiomio limestone caves. Our guide worked the farm where it was a treat to see glow-worms unspoiled by commercialism. We were nimble enough to navigate these caves, balancing precariously on a winding narrow ledge above the river below. The guide delighted in telling us about a Japanese visitor who had come through decked out in her high heels and coiffured hair. A strong wind swept through the cave and blew her wig into the river below, along with her pride. We were grateful not to be swept off the ledge as well.

American Honeymoon

Our honeymoon continued on the Hawaiian island of Oahu with a three-day stopover on our flight from New Zealand to Florida. We stayed at the historic Moana hotel on the beachfront of Waikiki. Exhausted after the long flight and emotional farewell to my family and friends, we slept to the soft purr of the rolling surf. Once refreshed, we toured the Polynesian Cultural Center's re-creation of seven South Pacific villages—Tonga, Fiji, Hawaii, the Maquesas, Tahiti, Samoa, and New Zealand. In the Hawaiian village, the chief serenaded us with the "Hawaiian Wedding Song" that Elvis Presley sang in the 1961 film *Blue Hawaii*. The same song was later dedicated to us and another honeymoon couple at a luau we attended at the Pink Palace.

Our Oahu leis made of fragrant yellow ilima flowers put us both in the mood for romance, though our ideas of how to achieve this were quite different. I thought it would be romantic to walk back to our hotel along the beach. Bobby preferred to walk on the sidewalk along the main road. As a Floridian, Bobby saw no special attraction in traversing sand and surf, but wanting to please his bride, he agreed.

I was ready to walk barefoot and enjoy the warm water caressing our feet, while Bobby preferred wearing his shoes and socks, suit and tie, in the style of an English gentleman. Thus, he was reluctant to go anywhere near the water because he did not want to get his shoes wet. Again, for the sake of his bride, he not only took off his shoes and socks, but he also walked with me hand-in-hand as the water lapped our feet. He even perked up when the skyline of Waikiki and Diamond Head presented a perfect backdrop for him to photograph me in the sparkling water.

Soon thereafter, romance and perfection took a dive. With the roar of three waves piling one on top of the other, I let go of Bobby's hand, lifted my dress, and braced for the crashing waves. Regrettably, Bobby anticipated nothing—his first indication of trouble was when he found himself flailing prostrate in the swirling waves and clawing in the sand to resist the undertow threatening to pull him out to sea.

He wondered if I was looking for evidence of his demise when he heard me calling out, "Pass me your shoes! PASS ME YOUR SHOES!"

Of course, it was nothing so sinister. I had withstood the waves by digging my toes deep into the sand, but could do nothing to stop Bobby's plunge. My first thought was to salvage his shoes since he had been so adamant about not getting them wet.

I helped Bobby to his feet and noticed something far worse than wet shoes—salt water was streaming out of the camera case still hanging around his neck. His camera was ruined. I captured the moment on my cheap camera and titled the picture: Total Trauma. Somehow Bobby's photo of me on Waikiki Beach survived the salt water—our $200 picture represented the replacement cost of the camera, not the value of the subject matter. This was when I learned that a new camera was a nonnegotiable budget item. I did restrain Bobby from bringing the ruined camera on the plane in a bucket of water to prevent further corrosion.

Upon arrival to the US mainland, we spent time in Los Angeles and San Francisco relaxing with Bobby's friends and family. Brooke and Paul hosted us in Los Angeles where one of their friends gave me a one-dollar note of special significance. Skillfully folded into the shape of a ring, he shared the meaning: "You're number one and the only one in my life." This man had kept this promise to his wife for 29 years and challenged Bobby to do the same.

Harriet and Al were our first hosts in San Francisco. Bobby caught up on all the LPA happenings during his leave of absence as president. Next, the newlyweds of two weeks spent two days with the newlyweds of two months—Bobby's cousin Susan and her husband, Bob. It was a great opportunity for me to learn about his childhood. Even more information was gathered when we spent an evening with his cousin Gary, his wife, Kathryn, and their baby, Craig.

This family time also gave me a glimpse into future scenes of my own marriage. Bobby and Bob lost all track of time when they started repairing an antique radio. Susan and I cooperated until we learned that our assignment—standing on opposite sides of the room holding wires—had relegated us into antennae. That was our signal it was time to go to bed and leave them to it.

Susan and Bob drove us to a San Francisco Bay area LPA chapter meeting in a member's home. It would not have mattered that pouring rain and a flat tire caused us to arrive an hour late, except we were the guests of honor. We appreciated the chapter's gift of *Mary Ellen's Household Hints*. After the business meeting, Daniel—another engineer—regaled me with additional hints on how to understand and live with my engineer, a little comedic relief we all enjoyed.

Our time in San Francisco would not have been complete without a visit to Lombard Street, promoted as *the crookedest street in the world*. Designed in the 1920s, the eight sharp turns help traffic navigate the steep incline. Along with the beautiful flowers and fabulous view, it could also have been a picture of God's design for our life ahead with the many sharp steep turns, tremendous beauty, and wonderful outlook.

Chapter 4
Alien World

Angela's US Arrival

Our honeymoon ended with me alone in a windowless, sparsely furnished room. Thirty minutes passed before the door opened and an official entered to take my fingerprints and a mug shot. Despite the detention, I was not under arrest. Rather, I was entering the United States for the first time as a permanent resident alien and taking the final step in the process of emigrating from New Zealand to the United States. Once my passport was stamped, I was free to go and join Bobby who anxiously waited for me on the other side.

Transitions

Two weeks after our Florida wedding, we returned to Bobby's apartment in Arlington, Virginia, where a winter wake-up call greeted us. From the inside looking out, the snow piled high on either side of the sidewalk was beautiful, but it only took one step into a puddle of icy slush to convince this year-round-sandal-wearing girl that winter boots were a necessity. Thankfully my NZ sheepskin jacket insulated the rest of me well.

Adjusting to the climate change was one of the easiest transitions. Moving out of the spotlight into obscurity and from having a national reputation to only being known by my beloved was very difficult. Harder yet, Bobby went to work each day leaving me alone with no job, no friends, no family, and no church. Letters from home were a lifeline.

Domestic duties were now my primary occupation, and even those presented various challenges. Going shopping took much longer than expected. I did not know any of the brand names and spent much time reading labels to find what I wanted. In addition, I had never been much of a cook so outcomes were unpredictable—pea soup being a case in point. Bobby said he liked his pea soup thick and was surprised when I obliged with soup that was so thick you could stand your spoon up in it. We had enough left over to have re-fried soup for breakfast—which we skipped.

Language differences were such an adjustment that at times I wondered if Americans spoke the same language. Although people liked my NZ accent and we used the same words, people often did not understand what I meant. Here are a few examples:

- When Bobby did not get through on the phone, he was puzzled when I asked if the man was engaged. I should have asked if the line was busy.
- When I asked Bobby if he wanted cotton to tie the roast he was stuffing, he could not see how cotton would be of any use and asked instead for thread.
- When referring to an usher using a torch in a movie theater, people imagined a flaming fire instead of a flashlight.
- When saying we might need a brolly because it was spitting, people did not know to bring an umbrella because it was sprinkling.
- When asking guests if they would sleep on a lilo, they were hesitant to agree until they saw the air mattress coming out of the closet.
- When I asked for a biscuit with my tea, I got something that looked like a bun and tasted like a scone. I should have asked for a cookie.

Learning to drive on the right side of the road was only one of the necessary adjustments to driving in America. Bobby realized this when I stopped at a traffic light in the middle of the intersection. It made sense to me because I was under the light and there was no line marking a stopping point before the light. My excursions at the wheel usually ended with me getting lost.

In the first few years of our marriage, we often joked that Bobby and I got along so well because we were both aliens: he was from Jupiter and I was from New Zealand.

Tea Chest Shipment

On January 13, 1982, we had a driving adventure that was foreign to both of us. After getting notice that my tea chest shipment of personal effects had arrived at the Philadelphia port, we decided to pick up the items ourselves. It was actually a matter of principle when we learned that shipping from Philadelphia to Arlington—about 150 miles—was more than the cost to ship from Auckland, New Zealand to Philadelphia,

Pennsylvania—about 8,500 miles. Bobby made all the measurements and assured me that the tea chests would comfortably fit into the back of our Honda wagon.

After staying overnight in Philadelphia, we woke to discover a blanket of snow. The initial allure vanished after three hours of driving through the city streets of Philadelphia in the slush and ice to the shipping line office.

Of course, paperwork had to be completed before we could enter the shipping terminal. We were unprepared for the hostile response of the gate guard, who abruptly waved our Honda wagon out of the container truck line and denied us permission to enter until Bobby got out of the car and showed him our paperwork. Finally, our unlikely transit vehicle was granted entry.

The shipping clerk's office was the next stop. Again, service was denied—this time because the clerk could not see Bobby over the counter.

Bobby asked, "Is anybody there?"

The clerk replied "no."

Taking his cue from other truckers getting service, Bobby quickly adapted, slamming down our papers on the counter above his head and gruffly stating, "Shipping order to be picked up."

The result? Immediate action.

Ordinarily, trucks pick up shipments by backing up to the loading bay. We drove right inside the warehouse. Surrounded by rows and rows of floor-to-ceiling shelving filled with boxes, we had no idea how we would find my tea chests, let alone get them into the car. There were no workers in sight—until Bobby got out of the car, revealing his stature. Suddenly, workers appeared from all corners of the building, convinced that Bobby was a movie star or one of the millionaire real estate twins who were the same height and age as Bobby. Their assumptions—uncorrected by either of us—provided all the help we needed to locate and load the tea chests into our wagon. Just as Bobby had calculated, they fit with inches to spare.

Our three-hour ordeal at the terminal was almost over—or so we thought. I was driving towards a warehouse opening when Bobby yelled out, "STOP."

He was impressed and totally relieved that I responded instantly. I had jammed on the brakes just before launching off the loading bay ledge.

The whiteout of the continuous snowfall made it impossible to tell that this way out was for the birds.

My First Blizzard

Disaster averted, I backed out the warehouse entrance on level ground, and we started home. An hour-and-a-half later we had only travelled 10 miles, so we pulled off the highway and found a motel. Then we learned that not everyone had escaped disaster that day.

The snow blizzard had hit Washington and Air Florida flight 90 had crashed into commuter traffic on the 14th Street Bridge before sinking into the Potomac River. Seventy-eight people were killed—74 on the plane and four on the bridge. Within a half-hour of the plane crash, three more people died in a Metro derailment on the Blue/Orange Line. If Bobby had been in DC that day, he could have been in the traffic on the bridge the plane crashed into, or on the Orange Line going to Ballston Station in Arlington. God's hand was surely protecting us.

Our first Valentine's Day

Our first Valentine's Day together was supposed to be special—at least, that is what I was expecting. I gave Bobby a romantic card depicting a cartoon of a woman with curly hair lying under the bedcovers with an empty pillow next to her. The message read:

Bobby,
If you'd like to be my Valentine, you know where to find me.
All my love and kisses.
Angela

I anticipated my very first-ever Valentine's card in return. Instead, my tears overflowed when Bobby had no card to give me. It never occurred to this new husband—remember his analytical mind—that a wife would expect such a gesture. It was the one and only time he made this mistake.

Chapter 5
Baltimore Beginning

Dwarfism Medical Research

In April 1981, Bobby won the battle to be reinstated to his job at the Access Board, but he lost the war. The money was there to pay his salary but not to fund the communications research for which he was hired. As a result, after only one year with the federal government Bobby pursued another dream—to use his biomedical engineering education and talent for the benefit of little people. In April 1982, he embarked on dwarfism medical research for a nonprofit organization affiliated with Johns Hopkins Hospital in Baltimore.

Bobby would be tasked with compiling and analyzing the medical data. The plan was for the doctor to use the analysis to write medical publications on various types of dwarfism.

Bobby spent his first month on the job becoming familiar with the medical data and relevant literature. Two college summer interns assisted, saving him hours of tedious data entry into the computer. This allowed Bobby time to write the program needed for data analysis.

Loss of Health Insurance and the Unthinkable

Bobby sacrificed both a significant salary and the security of a steady paycheck for the challenge of working with a pioneering doctor that specialized in dwarfism. We were both willing to sacrifice part of his salary and the job security he'd had with the government, but were reluctant to lose our excellent health care coverage. After much discussion and medical consultation about the pros and cons of my becoming pregnant, we agreed it was too risky for me to have biological children. Just as difficult was the decision of who would take the permanent step to prevent a pregnancy from occurring. Bobby reluctantly volunteered.

Although we still had insurance when we met the urologist, it would expire before an available date for the procedure. Since paying out-of-pocket wasn't feasible, the urologist offered to do the unthinkable. He was willing to report falsely the procedure date to the insurance company to bring it within the period of insurance coverage. I did not believe in situational ethics and knew this was wrong. After I had lied to the hosts at the International Guest House a year earlier, I didn't want to take another step away from God's standard of truth. I protested, but not enough to convince Bobby to decline the offer.

God did not strike us dead on the spot. But throughout the years, He put us on the receiving end of many instances of dishonesty and deception. The first instance occurred when the boy in the upstairs apartment stole Bobby's coin jar. It was disappointing, but only in hindsight did we realize that this was the beginning of many lessons God used to bring us to repentance and godly living. Meanwhile, we greatly benefited from God's amazing patience and provision for our needs.

Second Story Apartment

We rented a two-bedroom apartment close to the hospital for Bobby and law school for me. Bobby's sister, Paula, knew the building owner and was able to get us a reduction in the rent. Our apartment was on the second level in a 12-story building with an assigned parking space in the underground garage.

The closeness of our neighbors was a new issue for us. We were careful not to talk loudly in the hallways and avoided running the dishwasher late at night, so we were baffled when our downstairs neighbor complained about unexplained noises coming from our apartment. We finally narrowed it down to the noise made as we dragged the stool on the kitchen floor. We eliminated the disturbance by hiring a contractor to build a carpeted platform along the length of the counter. This not only stopped the offensive noise, but also the continual rigor of climbing on and off a stool.

Bobby happy at work on custom kitchen platform

Hospitality

LPA's mission to improve the quality of life for people with dwarfism is largely achieved through a network of little people and family members who support and encourage one another. For example, many members open their homes for local chapter meetings and welcome those visiting from out-of-town. We both enjoyed being hospitable, and LPA gave us plenty of opportunities to do so.

It did not take us long to develop our own brand of hospitality. After a grand tour of the apartment that included showing the location of food and supplies, guests were encouraged to make themselves at home. We did not have the time or energy to wait on people. It followed that overnight guests would pitch in with meal preparation and cleanup.

Our first opportunity for hospitality in Baltimore came after the April 1982 International Conference for Little People held in Washington, DC. We were pleased to host friends from New Zealand as well as delegates from Australia, England, Germany, and Sweden.

Our proximity to Johns Hopkins Hospital allowed us to offer shelter to LPA families of hospital inpatients or outpatients returning for follow-up appointments. The special adaptations we'd made to our apartment also gave parents ideas on how to modify their homes for their child with dwarfism.

A couple in our local LPA chapter reached out to us to help their son who was having difficulty adjusting to his size. Bobby responded by planning a boys' weekend retreat at our apartment. Two of the three boys who attended had spondyloepiphyseal dysplasia (SED), the same type of dwarfism as Bobby. The boys all enjoyed being able to reach the counter from our kitchen platforms and were right in there helping Bobby cook breakfast. We spent a relaxing afternoon at the apartment swimming pool, ate pizza for dinner, and went to see the movie *Star Trek II: The Wrath of Khan*.

Billy—the inspiration for the retreat—had started the weekend making excuses every time he was asked to do something, "because he was the smallest."

Well, in the company of five little people he'd definitely picked a losing argument. By Sunday, he seemed to have an improved perspective and had stopped making any references to his size. We cannot take credit for how well Billy turned out as an adult, but later—more than 25 years later—we learned that the retreat had made a definite impression on him.

We assumed our invitation to the wedding of Mr. Bill Klein and Dr. Jennifer Arnold was extended by the bride who'd been the flower girl at our Florida wedding in November 1981. Imagine my surprise when I introduced myself to the groom who recalled specific details of that boys' weekend. "Billy" had grown up to own a successful business and is a star on TLC's reality show, *The Little Couple*. Who could have imagined that the two children whose lives we separately touched in Florida and Maryland would meet as adults and fall in love?

Visits from my NZ family were always welcome. My brother, Greg, stayed for five weeks with his two friends from Australia as part of their trip around the world. Their visit overlapped with a brief visit from my father and a cousin-in-law. We were all together to celebrate our first wedding anniversary with the tradition of eating the top layer of the wedding cake. The fruitcake sealed in royal icing and stored in the freezer tasted just as good as it did on our wedding day.

Return to Law School

When I accepted Bobby's marriage proposal and agreed to live in the United States, I knew it would require my return to law school for at least one year. In order to practice law in the US, I would need to hold the American juris doctorate (JD) degree and pass a state bar exam to qualify for a license to practice law in that state. The alternative was to study for a master's law degree at a District of Columbia law school, take the DC bar, practice law in Washington for several years, and then seek admission to a state bar based on reciprocity.

Once we settled on Baltimore as our residence, studying for a master's degree in the capital was not an attractive option. The hour-and-a-half commute each way, the higher tuition fees, and the need to continue working in DC after graduation were all negative factors. I opted for the JD and applied to the two law schools in Baltimore—the University of Maryland and the University of Baltimore.

I was relieved when both schools agreed to waive the Law School Admission Test (LSAT) since it measured skills that are essential for success in law school. I convinced them that I had demonstrated these skills with my bachelor of law degree from the University of Auckland School of Law and five years of law practice in New Zealand.

Both law schools accepted my application for admission in the spring of 1982. I chose to attend the University of Maryland School of Law because of its higher ranking and longer history. I did appeal their decision to only offer me one-third credit for my NZ law degree, and met with the assistant dean to negotiate for two-thirds credit. Although this dean did not offer much hope for the school revising its decision, he did inform me of my right to bring a petition for review to the admissions committee. He also warned me that I would be wasting my time because he was the chair of the committee and he did not foresee a different outcome. I told him it was my time to waste.

When presenting my petition, I addressed the committee members with the same respect given to an appellate panel of judges.

At the end of the review hearing, the committee member who appeared to have the greatest influence on the other members commented, "Well, you do act like a lawyer."

What did he expect from someone with thousands of court hours under her belt?

Despite the assistant dean's prediction, I did persuade the committee to change its decision. I did not get the two-thirds credit I wanted, but the committee met me half way and gave credit for half my NZ law degree. This reduced my law school attendance from four semesters to three.

The finances of returning to law school were a definite challenge. Bobby had taken an $11,000 pay reduction, I had been unable to get a temporary job, and the tuition was more than we had saved. Thus, we were extremely grateful when LPA granted me an educational scholarship of $500. We had the $2,000 saved to pay the nonresident fee in the first semester and the scholarship stretched to pay half my tuition in the second semester when I was eligible for the residential rate of $950.

Seven years after my NZ graduation from law school, I did not envision myself back in a classroom. Yet on August 23, 1982, I resumed student status. For me, it was something to endure, not enjoy. Any accomplishment achieved as a lawyer was of little consequence when faced with three hours of class a day and seemingly endless hours of reading and studying.

After the first few days, I doubted I was going to make it. Although the professors and facilities were excellent, the pressure was enormous. It was also difficult to connect with students when I was juggling required classes across all three years of study. The students were polite, but highly competitive, stressed out, and aloof. Many talked of dropping out.

The law school did their part by providing me with the reasonable accommodations of parking, an elevator key, a locker and mailbox within my reach, and a stool in the library. I used a luggage carrier to tote my books, but the books were so heavy that the carrier handle cracked under the strain. After a couple of weeks, I learned how to deal with the mental and emotional strain without also cracking.

Adjusting to the Socratic style of teaching—where professors teach by asking questions from the assigned reading pages—was daunting. It did not matter how much reading I had done, I lived in fear that the professor would call on me to comment on an obscure side note—not an environment in which I thrive. Thankfully, by the second semester, I was more confident, better organized, and more discerning as to how much time to invest in each course.

And then there were exams. One exam, in one sitting, to reveal everything learned in the entire semester is typical of law school, at least in the first year or two. I hated it. So, I elected to write a paper for credit wherever it could substitute for an exam. It may have been more work, but the outcome did not rest on a single performance that did not reflect how much I knew or understood. Besides, I always enjoyed research and writing and it allowed me to choose subjects that were of interest to me. For example, a paper comparing the legal aid systems in New Zealand and the US was an easy decision for a former NZ legal aid lawyer. Also, eight years before the federal Americans with Disabilities Act protected people with disabilities from discrimination, I wrote a paper on disability employment discrimination in Maryland.

Chapter 6
Fundraising and Principle

Grant Funding

When Bobby accepted employment with the nonprofit organization on dwarfism research, we knew we would be involved in fundraising. Grant dollars funded Bobby's salary and the initial grant would end in six months. As a result, I utilized the Foundation Center in Washington, DC, to sift through thousands of foundations to find the few focused on medical research.

The next step was to write the actual grant requests, a huge volunteer task that required 100% effort. It resulted in 81 initial requests for funds, two small grant donations, and lots of waiting. We lived in hope of landing *the big one* that would support the research and Bobby's job.

Direct Mail Letter

The doctor directing Bobby's research recruited a retired marketing executive to write a draft letter intended for a direct mailing to research organization supporters. The letter featured both of us, but was so far off base we did not even recognize ourselves. It was clear that the writer knew nothing about little people—much less Bobby or me personally. Indeed, his fundraising philosophy was to tug at the emotional purse strings of the intended donors. The letter was loaded with images of dependency, distress, exaggerations, and offensive words—victim, crippled, plight, and suffering. Bobby was portrayed as a pitiful poster child type needing to be rescued from pain and the jaws of death. The depiction was of a patient, not a professional. There was no mention of his success as a biomedical engineer with a master's degree coming to the organization to do medical research.

When we refused to endorse the letter, the only positive change was the removal of the fictional story about me—the pity-party philosophy still dominated. We discussed our concerns with the doctor and he agreed to meet with us and the letter writer. However, on the date set for the meeting, the doctor was unavailable and sent his assistant in his place. We explained that such fundraising tactics cause little people to be pitied and patronized. In turn, such misrepresentations hinder any conception of little people as equal contributing members of society.

At the same time, we presented a philosophy that would preserve Bobby's dignity and show his success. We argued that donors respond to knowing that their contribution is a worthy investment in a people with ability, determination, resilience, hope, and a future. Clearly, the writer was hearing such ideas for the first time. We hoped he could see that our philosophy and his letter were incompatible. Yet the next draft of the letter was virtually unchanged.

The doctor shut down our discussions with the letter writer and met with us separately. He appeared to understand our concern, but that understanding never translated into changed words on the page. Despite numerous attempts to reach common ground, all draft letters continued with the emotional appeal for funds. Bobby could not agree to this use of his name and person. It was a matter of principle.

As Benjamin Franklin said, "If principle is good for anything it is worth living up to."[1]

Unfortunately, our stand on principle had caused an early rift in the working relationship between Bobby and the doctor. Bobby had come to the nonprofit to improve the lives of little people—he could not endorse a letter that would encourage potential donors to view little people as helpless victims dependent on charity.

Eventually the nonprofit gave up seeking Bobby's endorsement of the letter. But this wasn't the end of the matter. Trust was completely broken when the nonprofit mailed the letter without Bobby's knowledge or permission.

Family and Church Support

We needed some time-out after the distress created by the secret mailing of the fundraising letter demeaning Bobby's name and achievements. The break came as a Christmas gift from Bobby's mother and sister, Paula—airline tickets to Florida. We had three great weeks to enjoy Christmas and the 1983 New Year celebrations, sunshine, and family.

There's nothing like a mother's touch

It also gave us time to rest, reflect, and recognize that any future with the nonprofit would not fulfill Bobby's dream of using his biomedical engineering education and talent for the benefit of little people.

Our Christian faith was a critical support that helped us through the demands of work and law school. Upon our return from Florida in January 1983, we were finally successful in finding a church family at the Second Presbyterian Church in Baltimore. It was a large church where we enjoyed the service, the choir, the people, and the minister. Despite their gracious intent to make us comfortable, we declined the offer to build us a custom footrest. They did insist on reserving a front-row pew for us.

Within two weeks of our first church attendance, Reverend Smart made an unannounced home visit. We were shocked because this was February of 1983—when almost 23 inches of snow covered the city after the second biggest snowstorm on Baltimore's record books. But the Reverend, well used to harsh climate conditions in Scotland, walked the half mile from the church to our apartment. It was a safe assumption that he would find us at home. I especially appreciated his visit after learning that, like me, he was an alien resident and a former practicing attorney. We benefited from the reminder that despite the storms of life, God always shows us a way through.

Good News, Bad News

After more than a year of my volunteer grant-writing for the nonprofit, the long-awaited break finally came. A well-endowed national foundation approved a grant to fund medical research for a specific type of dwarfism. The check was in hand and the vital research could continue. At least that is what should have happened. Bobby went off to the nonprofit board meeting prepared to celebrate. I stayed at home to study in final preparation for law school exams.

The board was definitely excited to have received the foundation check. Organization funds were low and this grant presented as the answer for paying staff salaries. However, the board did not take kindly to Bobby's insistence that the funds were restricted to the research as described in the grant. They agreed with the doctor that they had the discretion to spend the grant money as they pleased. The good news had definitely turned into bad.

Bobby had three choices: (1) work contrary to the grant purpose; (2) resign; or (3) face discharge.

Bobby chose to resign. He came home from the meeting and was almost inconsolable as he knelt on the floor and sobbed into my lap. The doctor had not only directed the board how to act, but he also had insulted us both when he told Bobby that he had changed since he married me. Bobby resented the wedge the doctor tried to place between us. If there was any change in Bobby, he had developed the courage to stand up for what was right.

I was so thankful for the stance he was taking. Nonetheless, it was a tremendous strain on both of us. My law school exams would begin in a few days and studying under these circumstances was extraordinarily difficult. Bobby was heartbroken. Not only did he lose his dream job, he also lost his friendship with the doctor. When the doctor tried to salvage the relationship by sending flowers to our apartment, it was as though they were for a funeral. The accompanying note expressing the desire for the friendship to survive this time of sorrow and tribulation was hollow, given that the doctor had inflicted the sorrow.

In one sense, the breakup seemed sudden; yet, in another, we knew after all the fuss about the fundraising letter that a parting of the ways was inevitable. We were just surprised at the timing. The level of dishonesty compelled us to seek independent counsel. Our first advisor was a former editor of a foundation magazine. This advisor told us that Bobby had a legal duty to inform the foundation of the change in circumstances. When Bobby advised the foundation of his resignation, the funds to the nonprofit were frozen. This is when the nonprofit learned that indeed they did not have the discretion to use the grant money as they pleased.

Our second advisor was the director of the Legal Services Clinic at the University of Maryland School of Law. While I was at the law school taking exams, this experienced attorney met with Bobby, the doctor, and the nonprofit attorney to negotiate Bobby's severance agreement. As a result, our interests were well protected.

A Budding Tomorrow in Midnight

Although I wondered if God was allowing all this to happen to discipline us for our own dishonesty in the past, I also knew that God had previously moved us to take pre-emptive measures. As the poet John

Keats wrote, "There is a budding tomorrow in midnight."[2]

Soon after the *midnight* of the fundraising mailing behind Bobby's back in December 1982, Bobby began searching for another job. By the time of his resignation four months later, he already had a full-scale job search underway.

By the beginning of May 1983, Bobby had a job interview lined up in Cleveland, Ohio, while I was taking my law school exams. A week later, Bobby accepted a job offer as a rehabilitation engineer at a hospital in Cleveland. We saw the bud in tomorrow and were well aware that God was guiding us through the other side of the storm.

We still had a deep sense of loss.

But as our friend George so rightly said, "You have to go where you can put bread on the table."

The hardest thing for me in leaving Baltimore, as it was in leaving New Zealand, was leaving friends. However, the blow was softened because most of these friends were members of LPA that we would continue to see at events over the years.

On June 4, 1983, we hosted our official farewell—an open house from 1:00 p.m. until 11:00 p.m. Apartment living made it necessary to spread out the guests and a come-and-go event gave us a better opportunity to spend one-on-one time with people. We exchanged thoughtful reminders of each other as some brought us gifts and I gave away plant clippings.

The sentiments expressed in cards and notes like these touched us deeply:

Life wouldn't be half as nice without friends . . . ~Norma and Richard

Good friends are never far apart. ~Betty and Charlie

Here's the saddest goodbye that has ever been said . . .

but the gladdest of wishes for good times ahead. ~Robin

Chapter 7
Cleveland Changes

Getting Established

We had moved three times—from Arlington to Baltimore to Cleveland—in our first 18 months of marriage. All the changes left us feeling more like newbies in marriage boot camp than a well-adjusted couple. We hoped that we had completed our basic training and there would be no more upheavals ahead.

The move to Cleveland, Ohio, was an opportunity for Bobby to give up his childhood name and take on his proper name of Robert. Len Sawisch, a psychologist friend and LPA member, had planted the seed about a year earlier after sharing that he ditched his nickname of Lenny to fit his professional profile. The church across the street from our apartment was called St. Roberts, so naturally we had to check it out. It was a good thing, because the message on the day we attended had our names written all over it. More accurately, the name of the doctor whose actions had cost us dearly was engraved on both of our minds as we listened to the lesson on forgiveness.

We left church that day sharing our thoughts, and agreeing with the words of William Blake, "It is easier to forgive an enemy than to forgive a friend."[1] Only through God's love would we eventually be able to forgive the doctor.

Meanwhile, we forged ahead with all that Cleveland had to offer. Once again, we chose multi-level apartment living with underground parking. This time, however, we were on the 14th floor with a balcony, a lake breeze, and a sunset view of Lake Erie and the Cleveland skyline.

It was quite a change from our second-floor apartment in Baltimore. We discovered this when the fire alarm went off on our first day in the apartment. Surrounded by our 72 unpacked boxes of possessions we hoped it was only a false alarm. It was not. As the fire engines pulled into the driveway, Robert called the office to see if we needed to evacuate. Ordinarily a blaring fire alarm would make this a ludicrous question, but as the elevator would be off-limits in a fire, we knew we could not make it down the stairs on our own. Thankfully, the car explosion in the parking garage was quickly controlled, the alarm was turned off, and we were able to stay in the apartment. For future emergencies we were instructed to go to the stairwell and walk up two flights where we would be rescued from the roof. The likelihood of such a rescue seemed just as remote as the trouble that lay ahead.

Other than the initial alarm in high-rise living, we were able to adjust the apartment for our convenience. We modified the kitchen using the platforms from Baltimore to fit the smaller kitchen and Robert installed the telephones. The wall hangings had to wait until we recruited helpers at the open house we hosted for Robert's co-workers.

When Robert crossed the threshold of the Cleveland Metropolitan General Hospital, he was inducted into the white coat brigade. This job was a shift from medical research as a biomedical engineer into clinical practice as a rehabilitation engineer. In this position, Robert's job involved improving the independence of individuals with disabilities through environmental changes and adaptive equipment.

Robert was part of the medical team that saw patients in the clinics for spinal cord injury, comprehensive care, and arthritis. He thoroughly enjoyed the collaboration with other engineers and doing hospital rounds with the physicians. He gained a lot of satisfaction when people with disabilities benefited from the devices he recommended, modified, or built from scratch. Much of Robert's work involved providing alternate access to computers, environmental control units, and wheelchair controls. The 777-bed hospital was so large that Robert had to use a wheelchair to travel from his office, to the laboratory, and around the facility.

The Blessing of New Friends

We were also blessed with many new friends in Cleveland. Robert settled into a routine of eating lunch at the hospital with a fellow rehabilitation engineer and a medical photographer. This grew into an occasional social meal with spouses and even a sailboat ride on Lake Erie. Robert's two-year term as president of LPA meant we did not come into Cleveland as strangers. Many local little people knew us by reputation and opened their hearts and homes to us. Sharing meals and good times together became our new normal, and we also learned from each other—how to improve on our home modifications and even our marriages.

Barbara and Ed had been married 20 years, so I paid attention when Barbara told me something, although I couldn't believe it was true: "The things that annoy you about Robert today will still annoy you 20 years from now."

In other words: *Accept him as he is because he is not going to change! She was right.*

Our friendship with Jim and Kathy began through the Texas Instruments (TI) users' group. We had been TI users for a year because of a generous discount from Lee Kitchens, an LPA icon and TI Executive. Robert and Jim had regular phone discussions about their computers, and since Jim only lived about a mile away, we often got together with the whole family. One time when Kathy was away, I made a flaming impression on Jim and his son, Chris. Just as they buzzed from downstairs to announce their arrival, the dinner caught on fire. The flames flashed from the oven at the same time as Robert greeted them at our apartment door. I avoided using the fire extinguisher, and salvaged the dinner, but for some reason Jim wanted us to eat at his place after that.

LPA Activities

As immediate past president of LPA, Robert was still a member of the LPA Board of Directors that met at the annual meeting in Boston, Massachusetts, in July, 1983. We enjoyed the convention week along with 420 other delegates. Some especially enjoyed razzing Robert who not only debuted his new name, but also a new look in the convention brochure. In the gallery of national officers, Robert sported a snorkel and goggles in contrast to the formal attire of the other officers. I had submitted two photos—the funny one for the committee's personal pleasure and a serious one for publication. The committee decided to share the joke with everyone.

The North Coast LPA chapter in Cleveland received its charter. As a result, we became charter members along with approximately 40 others who attended the first official chapter meeting on August 13, 1983. As active members: we hosted a chapter meeting in March 1984; I became editor of the chapter newsletter; and we worked on the planning committee for the District 5 Spring Regional in Cleveland. The regional was enjoyed by over 100 little people and their families from Indiana, Kentucky, Michigan, Ohio, and West Virginia.

Maryland Law Degree

With Robert well situated, I turned my attention to my own career. I still had one semester of law school to complete my American law degree. We initially thought I would stay in Baltimore to finish my studies while Robert started his job in Cleveland 360 miles away. Thankfully, when I presented my dilemma to the chair of the administrative committee, he said they were not so callous as to expect a husband and wife to live separately. The committee agreed for me to study at an ABA-approved law school in Cleveland for credit toward my Maryland law degree. In other words, even though studying at a law school in Cleveland I would still graduate with a University of Maryland law degree. This was so much more than I had dreamed. God showed me another timeless truth:

[He] . . . is able to do far more abundantly beyond all that we ask or think. ∞ *Ephesians 3:20*

At the beginning of my third decade on the planet, I did my final semester of law school at Cleveland-Marshall College of Law, a division of Cleveland State University. For the most part, things worked out well with carpooling, friendly students, and reasonable accommodations. The law library bought the best stool I have ever seen; it had wide steps, hand-rails, and a platform at the top.

Nonetheless, I was surprised in one class to learn that cheating was common. For example, one professor had not changed his writing assignment in years and many students would copy from someone who took the class the year before. The partner with whom I was paired wanted us to do the same. She was upset when I insisted that we do original work. She went along reluctantly until we earned an *A* instead of the *B* on the paper she had planned to copy. My 1984 started off well with graduation from the University of Maryland Law School.

Visiting Family and Friends

For Christmas 1983, we drove the 300 or so miles to Robert's relatives in Munster, Indiana. We enjoyed ourselves despite the December 25th headline in the Chicago Tribune:

25 below! It's misery [2]

Despite shivering in the dangerous, record-breaking cold, Robert went horseback riding in a barn with his cousin Carolyn; the horses needed the exercise to stay alive.

When it was time to go home, our car would not start. The oil had frozen! After waiting hours, the tow truck that finally came broke down and was towed away by a second tow truck. We did not get on the road until 6:00 p.m. Our picnic lunch became dinner and we finally arrived back in Cleveland at 1:00 a.m. where the weather had warmed up to 12°F. We had kept ourselves alert on the drive home by listening to Ohio bar review tapes on criminal law.

We rang in the New Year of 1984 with several friends from Services for Independent Living in Euclid. We gathered at Kathy's house with our food, hats, and noisemakers. As midnight approached, we realized that the glasses for a toast were in a cabinet out-of-reach to all six wheelchair users. Robert obliged by climbing up and standing in the sink so he could get the glasses from the cabinet. The camera flashes of Robert's feat served as both our fireworks and fuel for our laughter.

Ohio Bar Exam

I was too busy studying for the Ohio bar exam—coming up at the end of February—to celebrate my law school graduation in January. The exam was in Columbus, three hours south of Cleveland. Because we only had one car, Robert had to drive me to Columbus on the weekend, leave me at a motel near the exam site, and drive back to Cleveland for work on Monday.

I awoke on Monday morning to see snow falling—nothing unusual about that in an Ohio winter. However, to wake up on Tuesday—the first of three exam days—and still see snow falling was alarming. I had prepared for the exam with endless hours of study, but had not prepared for a blizzard that dumped about 12 inches of snow. My fear was that my pre-ordered cab would be a no-show. If I did not get to the exam site on time, locked doors would keep me from taking the exam for another six months.

I thanked God when cabs came for me at both the beginning and end of the day. It was a blessing to meet Yvonne and Paula at dinner in the restaurant across the street from the motel. They recognized me from the exam site and invited me to join them. We encouraged one another and diligently returned to the motel for another night of last-minute study.

I would never have made it back to the motel without their help. They held onto me—one on each side—to stop me slipping and sliding in the snow and ice. When blocked by a wall of snow left in the wake of a snow plow at the motel driveway, a motel employee shoveled the snow and helped lift me over the snow bank. Preparing for such obstacles was not in the bar review material.

It was definitely a God-ordained bonding experience with Yvonne and Paula. The three of us teamed up for the next two days for ongoing support, meals, and rides. Our meal the second night at the Spaghetti Warehouse had perked up our spirits and given us the energy to get through the last grueling exam day. We made a pact, that if we all passed the bar, we would return there for a celebration meal after the swearing-in ceremony in May.

On May 2, 1984, I woke up at 6:45 a.m. in a cold sweat. It was the day to call in for the bar exam results and I dreamed that I had failed.

When the operator reported excitedly, "You passed!" I was relieved to learn that not all dreams—or nightmares, in this case—come true.

I was just as excited to learn that my bar-exam friends, Paula and Yvonne, had also passed.

The timing worked out for my sister, Deborah; brother-in-law Rob; niece Nadia; and their friend Lucky to join us in Columbus when I was sworn in as a member of the bar of the Supreme Court of Ohio. As agreed in February, our luncheon celebration included Paula, Yvonne, and their spouses at the Spaghetti Warehouse.

Family Visits from Down Under

Three weeks with my sister and family was a welcome reprieve from my job search. Our first time meeting 18-month-old Nadia was her first time finding everything in our apartment within reach. The kitchen was her favorite place despite one nasty fall between the platforms. After a few days in Cleveland, we rented a car and took a ten-day road trip. Niagara Falls was our first stop. We were all enthralled with the view and power of the falls from the Maid of the Mist vantage point. The two Roberts captured it all on camera—or so we thought. My brother-in-law Rob was later horrified to find his camera had no film in it. We were relieved that Robert's photos recorded the occasion for us all.

Rob, Lucky, and Deborah did all the driving on our road trip. Rob and Lucky loved the open highways and clicked into racing mode. Robert repeatedly warned them that such high speeds would eventually cause us to be pulled over and fined on the spot. I warned that when it happened, we would not be paying the fine out of our travel fund. The inevitable happened in South Carolina. We all heard the whirr of a siren and saw the flashing red light. The irony was that Deborah—the slowest of the three fast drivers—was at the wheel. Lucky was fired up by the opportunity to meet a real live American Smokey of movie fame. He learned everything he wanted to know about the patrol car and posed for a photograph with the officer.

There was no racing at Daytona Beach, but we did enjoy driving the car on the beach with no fear of getting stuck in the sand. We made sure to get back on terra firma before the tide came in; failure to do so would have resulted in another fine and a tow truck fee to pull us out. Our next race was at Epcot and Disney World where Robert and I rented two manual wheelchairs. Our fast drivers were also fast wheelchair pushers; this time it was the sound and vibration of shuddering wheels that got them to slow down. In one of those slow times, we watched Donald Duck's 50th birthday parade. Robert still talks about the day Snow White spotted him in the crowd and planted a bright, red lipstick mark on his cheek. Did she think she had found one of her seven dwarfs? In contrast, Nadia was terrified of any of the characters approaching her.

The Kennedy Space Center was our final stop before spending time with Robert's family in Stuart, Florida. Nadia was not interested in the lunar landing or shuttle launching and preferred making her own history by going solo—eating an ice cream cone for the first time.

In our final four days together, we relaxed and visited many friends and relatives, highlighted by our two families meeting for the first time. We enjoyed every minute and reluctantly returned to our homes too far apart from each other.

Depressed Economy and Job Discrimination

With the February 1984 bar exam behind me and a two-month wait for the results ahead of me, I turned my attention to finding a job in a depressed economy. For every attorney job advertised, there were as many as 100 applicants! One new law graduate was so desperate to get her foot in the door that she took a job as a legal secretary. I hoped that my five-year NZ legal practice would give me an advantage. It did not. I had also hoped that passing the Ohio bar exam would stir up interest.

It did not.

In my 12-month job search, I submitted 500 job inquiries or applications. This only netted a handful of interviews and no job offers. Three of these interviews clearly stand out as employment discrimination. Six years prior to the Americans with Disabilities Act protection, I had no recourse.

In one instance, a glass window overlooked the waiting room. I suspected that the interviewing attorney saw me through the window and used this lead-time to plan how to deny me a position. In this legal clinic with an assembly-line approach to the work, he told me there were only 30 minutes in which to gain a client's confidence and he was certain I would not be able to do this. Relating my experience as a duty solicitor (legal aid lawyer) in the NZ District Court—where I only had five minutes to gain a client's confidence—did nothing to persuade him otherwise.

At another interview, someone walked through the waiting room and into the office where I was soon ushered for the interview. Again, the interviewing attorney had advance notice of my dwarfism. This attorney disrespectfully leaned back into his leather chair and put his feet on the desk. The only questions he asked were unrelated to the job or my work experience. When he finally put his feet on the ground, I knew he was about to wrap the interview and was not considering me for the position.

With nothing to lose, I let him know the transparency of his actions when I said something like this, "It appears that you are closing this interview without asking me one question about my qualifications and what I would bring to your law firm."

This startled him into a bolt upright position in his chair. He sheepishly asked me, "Well, what would you bring to the firm?"

It seemed like a pointless exercise since his mind was made up before I entered the interview room, but I went into sales mode and pitched my experience and credentials. My speech did nothing to dint his prejudice, but at least he learned that I knew he was a bigot.

In the third interview, I felt more hopeful about getting the job. The interviewing attorney disclosed that his sister was a little person and was quite open when talking to me. And yet—still no job offer. I concluded that his sister's limitations—whatever they were—probably influenced his decision not to hire me. He was unable to discern the different skill levels among little people.

One interview that could have helped me get a job came on a local television station. The interview was about LPA on the Cleveland show Morning Exchange. Ellie Jones and I did the interview together and Ellie encouraged me to mention my job search. As a result, a couple of attorneys agreed to meet with me even though they did not have a vacancy. One of these attorneys gave me a promising lead to a position as an administrative law judge with a state agency. The vacancy closed when the judge withdrew his resignation—or so I was told.

I expressed my disdain for disability discrimination in *Student Lawyer*, an ABA publication. After writing a letter to the editor on an ABA proposal amending law school standards as they affect students with disabilities, I accepted the invitation to write a full-length article instead. The $200 I was paid for the article could not have come at a better time. I had no idea that God was laying the groundwork for a career in writing.

History Repeats Itself
Meanwhile, Robert had no idea that his days working at the hospital in Cleveland were numbered. On September 28, 1984, he was shocked to learn that the funding for his position would end on December 31, 1984—six months earlier than expected. This dashed any hope of the program achieving the goal of self-sufficiency at the end of the two-year grant period. We could not believe that history was repeating itself.

We suspected that the cause of the premature end to Robert's position was—again—the result of a diversion of funding for purposes other than those described in the grant. As a result, Robert filed a grievance with the hospital grievance review panel. The process did not allow for any legal representation, but Robert could bring a hospital employee. When the chief of medicine accepted Robert's invitation to come to the hearing, the panel realized the need to take Robert's grievance seriously.

We had become acquainted with the chief of medicine because of his NZ origin. Only three months earlier, we had enjoyed time together watching slides of his walk on NZ's Milford Track. The doctor was not only concerned for Robert's fair treatment, but was also disturbed that funds from a major donor to the hospital had possibly been misused. The hearing did not get Robert his job back, but it did result in his compensation for the last six months of the grant period.

Now we were both looking for work. The only good thing about this was that our job search was no longer restricted to Cleveland. No way did we want to move, but with Robert's work being so specialized, another move seemed the only way we could both get work. Whichever of us found the best job offer, we agreed to move to that location only if an opportunity for the other was available.

Robert sent out 160 resumes nationwide, which only netted two interviews—one near Harrisburg, Pennsylvania and the other in Richmond, Virginia. The program manager for the rehabilitation engineering position in Harrisburg made it clear that she thought Robert was the most qualified applicant, but she didn't have the final say. I was invited to join Robert on his second interview with the program director to pick between the final two candidates. Once again, prejudice reared its ugly head. The program director complimented Robert on his LPA achievements, but never got around to job-related questions. The follow-up phone call about some obscure computer program that Robert was unfamiliar with confirmed our suspicions. The director salved his conscience by saying Robert was less qualified than the other candidate who knew the computer program—one that was only tangentially related to the job.

The job search continued.

A Welcome Diversion

The fall 1984 visit of my two NZ aunts—Nan and Evelyn—was a welcome diversion from the stress of our job woes. One of the highlights was a 1,000-mile car trip circling Lake Erie in the US and Canadian territory. We were all on a learning curve as we discovered new terminology, went motel-shopping, and experienced living history at the Greenfield Village in Dearborn, Michigan, where we rented 19th-century wheelchairs. Another first was developing the courage to walk out of an overpriced restaurant after being seated.

We were literally on top of the world in Toronto's CN Tower—which at that time was the tallest in the world. We contrasted city life with a visit to the African Lion Safari Park in Cambridge, Ontario. Even more memorable than the lions was the farmer at his mailbox when we asked him for directions; we feared that his false teeth would shoot straight out of his mouth as he laughed at the idea of lions roaming the landscape.

The power and beauty of Niagara Falls gave perspective to our struggles.

On our return to Cleveland, Nan and Evelyn gave valuable input on the first draft of my book, *Dwarfs Don't Live in Doll Houses*, and we were thrilled by a live performance of Yul Brynner in *The King and I*. Nan encouraged us to make our first visit to the Methodist church down the road. The uncertainty of our future deepened the sadness of Nan and Evelyn's farewell. The soft snow falling as we came out of church on Christmas Eve spoke of the wonder of God's creation and care for us.

Chapter 8
New York Beginnings

New Jobs

The spring of 1985 was about more than turning pages on the calendar. By March, we both had employment that involved relocating to Rochester, New York. I accepted a job as a legal writer with Lawyers Cooperative Publishing (LCP) and Robert became self-employed as the sole proprietor of Adaptive Living. We reluctantly made this move when no opportunities opened up for us in Cleveland.

LCP made the physical move easy by paying the moving expenses and five nights in a hotel during our apartment search. It took about 100 phone calls to find an affordable unit with level entry. We hated

Ready to write law books for lawyers

to exchange the Lake Erie view for one of four walls with windows so high that we could not see outside, but the trade-off was a three-mile commute to work, a carport next to our unit, no emergency evacuation concerns, and rent that allowed us to save money for a house down payment.

Emotionally, the move was much harder. After almost two years in Cleveland, we suffered the loss of more great friends. As far as our LPA family, the pain was somewhat eased by knowing that we would occasionally see one another at meetings. For others, 250 miles was not so far that we could not drive for visits now and then, but we knew those visits would be infrequent.

Despite the difficulty of pulling up stakes so soon, we did look forward to a fresh start. I had always been interested in writing, but never dreamed that one day I would make a living writing law books for lawyers. My official job title was associate editor and my first writing assignment was on immigration law, a subject on which I had first-hand knowledge.

Long before employers were required to provide reasonable

accommodations, I received two accommodations: one I needed, one I did not. Onsite parking was the accommodation I did need since I could not walk the distance from the public parking lot. Even though onsite parking was reserved for managers, the problem was solved when Kris—a newly promoted manager—offered me a carpooling arrangement that allowed me to park in her space.

The accommodation I did not need mysteriously appeared one day in the bathroom—the installation of a kindergarten height toilet! I was transported into the fantasy land of Goldilocks and the Three Bears: one for papa bear (wheelchair height), one for mama bear (regular height), and one for baby bear (my height).

At this point, I had been on staff for several months, I could not help but ask, "What does the company think I've been doing all this time when I needed to use the bathroom?"

No doubt the accommodation was well intentioned, but it made for good employee policy manual material: *Always ask the person with a disability before making an accommodation.* To top it off, the baby bear toilet was too low and actually more difficult for me to use. As a rehabilitation engineer, Robert knew this principle well, but he was new on the scene and no one sought his professional advice.

When we first moved to Rochester, Robert launched his rehabilitation engineering practice, Adaptive Living. He marketed himself and presented seminars to agencies and health professionals likely to benefit from his services. Pat, a vocational counselor at Vocational Education Services for Individuals with Disabilities (VESID), was instrumental in putting Robert and his business on the Rochester map. She supported his application to become a VESID contractor and was the first to refer clients to Adaptive Living for services.

More exposure for Adaptive Living came from a June 1985 feature article and photo in the local section of the Rochester *Democrat and Chronicle* titled, "The tall problems of little people."[1] In addition to covering the newly chartered New York Finger Lakes LPA chapter, the reporter—Eric Gunn—zoomed in on Robert's story as a charter member, national LPA president for the second time, and businessman.

Christmas Surprise

At Christmas 1985, we made a new addition to our family. I arranged for his surprise delivery to our door on Christmas morning. Robert named him Budgie. I said this was like naming a cat *Cat*, but Robert said it did not matter because Americans don't know that in New Zealand parakeets are called budgies.

Robert had always wanted a bird and the two became fast friends. Budgie and Robert shared the home office where Robert used the computer's speech synthesizer to teach his new companion to talk. Budgie kept Robert's spirits up in the many lonely hours of building his business and provided comic relief from the stress of the LPA presidency.

Leisure Activities

Robert and I made time for fun activities, but these were mostly associated with LPA meetings or work friends. Highlights included 18th century history in Kingston, New York, and also canoeing and fishing with Craig and Linda at Chautauqua Lake, New York. Robert and Craig had more fun digging for worms than fishing, and skiing didn't appeal to me since I don't enjoy being wet, cold, and flat on my back.

We both tried sailing with my co-worker, David. With Robert assigned to steer the rudder and me to tie the ropes while David unfurled the sails on top of the boat, we had a clear recipe for disaster. David was a new sailor, Robert could not see over the cabin to know what lay ahead, and I could not tie the ropes. Robert abandoned the rudder to help me with the ropes causing David to rush to the rescue when we headed dead center for a moored boat! Thankfully, David avoided a collision, just like he avoided ever inviting us to crew for him again.

Chapter 9

Home at Last

Expired Passport

When I left my NZ home and immigrated to the US, I never dreamed that it would be five years before I would return. Finally, in December 1986 we landed in Christchurch, NZ, with plans to sightsee in the Garden City and visit friends and family throughout the country. As the plane taxied to the airport terminal, my heart almost stopped when I looked at Robert's passport. It had expired! It never occurred to me that his American passport was only good for five years since my NZ one was good for ten.

Robert's view out the plane window might be all he was going to see of New Zealand on this trip, but how was I going to tell him? I quietly handed him his passport and decided it was best for Robert to hear the news from an official. This way his reaction would be completely unrehearsed.

As expected, the immigration officer checked and rechecked Robert's passport then looked down and said to him, "Did you know your passport has expired?"

Robert expressed such dismay that the officer was motivated to find a way to let him in the country. He asked us to step aside while he called the main immigration office in the capital of Wellington.

While we waited for an answer on his entry status, Robert asked if I would return to the United States with him.

The reality of his situation set in when I answered, "No."

Although the trip would not be the same without Robert, I was not ready to miss the family reunion at Whangamata. The fact that it's one of the most popular NZ beach resorts was incidental. It was more that I could not miss returning to my childhood summer holiday venue, and I would be meeting many new family members for the first time.

Thankfully, the immigration officer returned with good news. Robert could enter the country on the condition that he went straight to the US Consulate office in Christchurch to apply for a new passport. This put a crimp in our sightseeing plans, but at least we had time to paddle down the Avon River through the botanical gardens.

Car Rental Discrimination

Another problem occurred in my home town of Papakura, South Auckland. The car rental agency refused to give us the car we had reserved. Unfortunately, prior to our arrival my father told the agency that we were little people. The company contacted their head office in Australia to see if this was a problem. When Robert went in to sign for the car with my brother, Greg, and my father, the clerk's directive was not to rent the car to any little people. Greg's reaction was not conducive to negotiation, so Dad sent him outside. Robert and Dad persuaded the clerk to rent us the car, but Dad had to co-sign on the rental agreement.

Family Christmas at Whangamata

We were thankful to join the Muir clan in Whangamata in time for Christmas. The only thing missing on Christmas Eve was a Christmas tree. It was too late to go tree shopping so Greg and my brother-in-law Rob went out to get a tree on a dark country road. They returned with a beauty that impressed everyone. Well, at least Dad enjoyed it until he went to golf a couple of days later. He was livid and had a hard time believing Greg did not know the tree was from the golf course. Dad's grief was the inspiration for our Scruples game addendum question: "You are a member of a golf club. Your son chopped down a prized tree at the 18th hole near the roadside. Do you tell that the tree is in your living room?"

Our month in New Zealand passed too fast. We enjoyed every minute with family and friends—picnicking, swimming, fishing, canoeing, snorkeling, sharing the road with cows, visiting my cousin's goat farm, and qualifying as aerial volcanologists after flying over extinct volcanoes in Rotorua.

Home Ownership

Upon our return to Rochester, we graduated from apartment living to home ownership. Our weekend to move coincided with the LPA District 2 Regional in Rochester. As members of the organizing committee, we were grateful that it was Memorial weekend so that we could follow through on our commitment to the 150 in attendance. Fabulous weather multiplied the fragrance and beauty of the world's largest lilac collection at the annual Lilac Festival in Highland Park. Rochester residents learned about the event from Dianne Carraway's article in the *Rochester Times Union:*

Little People Group Wants to Show Size Isn't Everything [1]

It was a great boost to the New York Finger Lakes chapter hosting the event and a good public education piece.

On Memorial Day, we switched gears to coordinate the movers who had agreed to work on the holiday. As first-time homebuyers, we bought a modest two-bedroom 1950s home with a below market mortgage interest rate. The attached two-car garage eliminated the need to scrape snow and ice off the cars in the winter and the short driveway reduced the amount of snow shoveling. We made several home improvements: ceiling insulation; electrical wiring upgrades; a handrail and five low-rise steps over the three deep steps from the garage into the kitchen; a platform lift over the stairs to the basement; and a ramp at the front door.

For a year, we used the original kitchen with the platforms first built for our Baltimore apartment. The platforms were finally retired after a three-week visit from Eric, a NZ contractor friend. He ripped out the inaccessible cabinets even before he recovered from jet lag. With the help of our neighbor Marsha, Eric built the custom cabinet frames; inset a stovetop into one of the cabinets; painted, plastered, wallpapered, and replaced missing floor tiles. We could use our kitchen without climbing, finally! Who could quibble about the selection of mismatched floor tiles?

After Eric's departure, the cabinets were completed by one of Robert's clients. Robert's engineering acumen had empowered this visually-impaired carpenter to use assistive technology to access his computer and the client empowered us to use our cabinets by building pullout drawers and cabinet doors.

Snow covered the backyard when we first saw the house. Our young niece Juliette had a hard time understanding why we bought a house with a dead tree in the front. When the snow melted and new leaves sprouted in the spring, we wondered why we chose one with so many gardens. The former owner had enough vegetable gardens to feed the entire neighborhood and enough flowers to fill all the vases. We saw no way to manage it all. We were about to return most of the garden to lawn when David, one of my co-workers, made us an irresistible sharecropping offer. He would garden and we would share the crops. As a result, for two years our diet improved with an abundance of fresh beans, corn, cucumbers, eggplant, lettuce, rhubarb, tomatoes, and zucchini. When David moved to a place with his own land and no longer needed to sharecrop, we sized the garden down to tomatoes, peppers, and rhubarb.

Instead of hiring a contractor to mow the lawns, we bought a riding mower. It had a grass catcher that we could easily slide on and off and we added an extension to reach the foot pedal. Robert's job was to maintain the mower and mine was to ride it. I had never mowed lawns in my life and the novelty soon wore off. The hose kept disconnecting from the catcher and sprayed grass everywhere and the vibration from the mower distressed every joint in my body.

We primarily got to know our neighbors during outdoor activities. Mary was quick to tell me I was mowing the lawn in the wrong pattern. After hearing this a few times, I stopped turning off the engine to hear what she was saying and kept mowing with a smile and wave in her direction. Flo would help whenever she saw us doing something outside. Sometimes she even helped when we were inside, by doing things like cutting our front hedge and taking out the garbage can.

Flo was not as knowledgeable about gardening as Mary. One day when Flo was helping Robert weed an overgrown flower garden, they started hacking at what looked like a dead bush. Mary helped me stop them from destroying a gorgeous lilac bush. Apparently, Robert should have paid more attention at the Lilac Festival.

In August 1987, the backyard with its garden and flowers was an excellent staging area for the surprise baby shower we had for two couples from my work. All 23 guests waited in the backyard for the arrival of Wayne and Jody, and Joel and Marguerite. Since we had recently moved to our home, the guests of honor were willing to survey the backyard before coming into the house, and were thrilled to get much more than a garden tour.

Church Home

After buying our physical home, we began looking for a church home. For me the spiritual awakening began with conversations and Bible studies with my co-worker, Beverly. However, Beverly's church was on the other side of town and Robert wanted to find a church closer to home. In our 18-month search, we attended Catholic, Presbyterian, Methodist, Lutheran, and Baptist churches. The denomination was secondary to finding a Bible-believing church that put their Christian faith into action.

All but one church fell short. A Catholic priest gave a financial report in place of his homily. A Presbyterian minister invited us to become church members without knowing if we were Christians. The Methodists were friendly, but the Bible was not central to their teaching. The Lutherans were uncomfortable with our short stature. Finally, at West Side Baptist one sermon got to me.

Pastor Barry repeatedly said, "If you don't feel close to God, guess who moved?"

I knew the answer to the question. The Holy Spirit moved me to join a ladies Bible study. Robert thought we should keep looking, but I had found my church home. My prayer was that Robert would also make it his.

Adaptive Living

Although our house was small, it had a full-sized dry basement. Moving Adaptive Living from a half-size bedroom into the basement gave Robert lots of room to spread out—he set up a secretarial station, a workbench, and storage area. After only two years in business, he had plenty of work within a two-hour radius. He would occasionally travel further, with one case taking him as far as Florida.

Robert marketed the business through seminars, service on various boards, and the media. For example, he lectured at the New York State Independent Living Conference. Bob Smith, the radio host of *Sound Bytes*, a radio talk show about computers, regularly invited Robert as a guest to discuss computer technology as it related to people with disabilities.

The Mayor of Rochester appointed him to serve on the Council on Disabled Persons: County of Monroe / City of Rochester. In March 1988, Robert was elected as chairperson of this council with the objective of removing social, resource, and environmental barriers limiting full participation of people with disabilities in the community.

One unexpected venture for Adaptive Living was the 1988 publication of my book, *Dwarfs Don't Live in Doll Houses*.[2] Robert helped with the layout, printer bids, and index. Although an artist friend designed the book cover, Robert was the photographer. It took three photo shoots on bitterly cold January days to get the right shot.

The shipment of 4,000 books was finally delivered the first week of April 1988. The marketing began at the LPA District 2 Regional in New Jersey and the local Authors' Day sponsored by the Friends of the Rochester Public Library. There was also a local newspaper article, a book party, and a book signing at two local bookstores.

International exposure followed when I gave the translation rights to Helga in 1990; she had bought the English version at the 1988 International meeting of Little People in Sydney, Australia. Despite my skepticism, Helga found a publisher for the German translation, *Jeder Mensch: Wird Klein Geboren Autobiographieeiner Kleinwuchsigen*,[3] and exhibited it at the Frankfurt Book Fair in Germany.

Chapter 10
Season of Travel

Florida Trips

In the first half of 1987, Robert traveled from Rochester, New York to Florida four times. I could only join him twice. These were not vacation trips, but rather to visit his mother whose lung cancer had spread to her bones. Paula had cared for Mother at home with only two brief hospital stays being necessary. Irene Van Etten left a big hole in the family when she died at age 73 on July 10, 1987.

As cousin Carol said, "She was kind and charitable; she knew what 'Love thy neighbor' meant and practiced it well."

Our trip to the funeral was a nightmare. Although we got a flight out of Rochester the same day as Mother died, we missed our connecting flight in Philadelphia. It was infuriating because we were at the departure gate on time. Unfortunately, during the 30-minute maintenance delay, we left the gate to get something to eat. Even though we returned to the gate within the half hour, the plane had already departed! Apparently, the plane was ready sooner than expected and we did not know you cannot hear boarding calls in restaurants. Although we got a flight to Atlanta that night, we did not make it to West Palm Beach until the next day. My four-page complaint letter to the airline resulted in an apology, reimbursement for our hotel, and a $150 check.

All of this traveling still played havoc on our budget, but Robert's brother Peter generously gave us $500 towards our cost of flying to the funeral. It was good that we were there to honor his mother and share in the family grieving process. Robert and his siblings were able to share one light moment when they watched Robert blow out candles on his birthday cake.

In September 1990, we began our Florida vacation with LPA friends in Orlando and then connected with my brother, Greg; his wife, Julie; and their daughter, Holly, visiting from Australia. We spent five days with Disney at the Polynesian hotel, the Magic Kingdom, Epcot Center, and MGM Studios. It was a highlight to see Holly hugging Minnie Mouse and Pluto hugging Julie.

We followed our time in Orlando with Robert's family in Lake Worth.

Greg drove the rental car. He did well driving on the right side of the road until he made what could have been a fatal turn. After a long day in Orlando and three hours on the road, Greg switched into autopilot at an intersection and turned onto the left side of the road, as is the custom in Australia. Traffic was coming straight at us and the median prevented Greg from pulling over to the right side of the road. Robert saw the escape route and told Greg to pull off the road into a plaza driveway. God protected us from disaster.

It was a relief to arrive safely and occupy ourselves with pursuits that did not cost money. Together we enjoyed tennis, volleyball, sightseeing, swimming, boating, picnics, and celebrating Holly's fifth birthday.

Upon returning to Rochester, we were ready to unwind from all the activity. Robert and I went back to work while the Muir family relaxed and shopped. Robert worked with Greg on his new computer, Greg mowed the lawns, and Julie cooked. On the weekend, we went to church, picnicked in a Lake Ontario park, and enjoyed Niagara Falls by sunlight during the day and laser lights at night. As always, the vacation ended before we were ready to say goodbye.

Philadelphia, Pennsylvania

In July 1987, we were in Philadelphia for LPA's 30th anniversary celebration. This time we avoided any airport drama by driving the 300 or so miles from Rochester, New York. If we had not been planning-committee members, we might have skipped the convention. However, this was not an option. Robert was the coordinator for the first LPA exposition of products and services for little people. We also had board meetings to attend, Robert as past president and me as the District 2 proxy. Nonetheless, we enjoyed the convention along with 836 other delegates. In addition to the traditional fashion and talent shows, there was an exhibition by Dancing Wheels with Mary Verdi-Fletcher. The highlight was the New Year celebration in July with the Philadelphia Mummers.

Boston, Massachusetts

In June 1988, Robert flew to Boston, Massachusetts. It was not the first time he had gone out of town on business, but this trip was different: it was for his movie-acting debut! Robert had a *blink-and-you-miss-him* part in an HBO cable movie called, Lip Service. The movie starred Griffin Dunne and Paul Dooley and received three stars in the TV Guide. It first broadcast on October 17, 1988. It was a very depressing movie about a washed-up television journalist being hustled for his job by a youthful, less-talented, ambitious upstart. Robert was one of the people interviewed by the veteran journalist. Despite his rookie status, he dared to give advice to the director. Surprisingly, the director made Robert's suggested change in the script, but in the credits retained the highly offensive description of his character as *midget.*

Australian Family in Rochester and Iowa

In 1988, we enjoyed eight excellent days in Rochester with my sister, Deborah; brother-in-law Rob; and their children, Nadia and Ashley. We had to fit the fun around our work schedules, but had time for Fourth of July fireworks, shopping, going to Lake Ontario beach, and picnicking at Letchworth Park. The girls enjoyed riding in Robert's wheelchair, washing dishes in the kitchen sink at their height, and sitting inside the kitchen cabinets before the drawers were installed.

We continued our family visit in Des Moines, Iowa for three days at the LPA National Convention. Our last night together was supposed to be a family BBQ with a hayride and outdoor games. Instead, the Iowa drought ended with a deluge, and flooding caused our bus to conk out en route to the farm. Deborah and Rob got drenched helping the bus driver get the bus started. The baked beans served in the leaking barn did nothing to compensate Deborah for sloshing through the rain and mud to take the girls to the toilet. I was upset when Robert and I were stopped from boarding the same bus back to the hotel as Deborah's family. We were in line together, but when the bus reached capacity, we were left behind to wait an hour and a half for another ride. Losing this precious time together was awful on our last night together before they flew home.

New York City and Ontario Canada

Robert had a sibling visit next when Paula; her husband, David; and their children, Juliette and James, came to New York in September 1988. Juliette and Paula had won the Florida Mother/Daughter Tennis Tournament and made it to the national semi-finals. We joined them at the Metropolitan Art Museum, Trump Plaza, the Empire State Building, and for a carriage ride in Central Park.

Paula and James spent the next week with us in Rochester. Two-year-old James had a great time reaching everything and picking fresh vegetables every day. We visited Niagara Falls and the orchard of Paula's friend Shirley in Ontario, Canada. Shirley filled our trunk with pears, apples, plums, and grapes, and we successfully crossed the US/Canadian border without inspection delays or tariff payments.

Australia and New Zealand

Robert went to Australia and New Zealand on a World Rehabilitation Fellowship for six weeks in April and May of 1989. As much as I wanted to go with him, being limited to two weeks of annual leave made that impossible. After visiting more than 50 sites, Robert could boast that he had seen more of the two countries than me. His fellowship was a study of how high-technology equipment is selected and used by people with disabilities.[1] The ingenuity of the professionals impressed him, but he was disappointed not to find a job or business opportunity Down Under. Not wanting to miss out completely, I flew over for one week in New Zealand before joining him for his last week in Australia.

One of many airport family farewells

In addition to family time, Deborah had organized and joined us in Melbourne, Victoria, for a television interview on *The Bert Newton Show* to promote *Dwarfs Don't Live in Doll Houses*. The book promotion continued in Baltimore, Maryland, at the annual LPA conference in July 1989. Two news articles were a definite boost to sales.

Little People's Biggest Problem: Small Mind

In No Small Feat, She Finds True Stature as a Writer[2]

The trip Down Under caused me to cut my time at the conference back to a four-day weekend. I returned to work and Robert continued his conference duties. When he checked out of the hotel at the end of the week, he was surprised to see an expensive champagne brunch for four charged to our room. He knew he hadn't so indulged and was almost sure I had not, either. He questioned the bill, but paid it because I was not there to ask.When Robert returned from the conference, he confirmed that I had not made this room charge and asked the hotel to remove it from his credit card. It took months for the hotel to concede that the signature on the charge to our room was fraudulent. Apparently, they had been busy investigating many such cases.

England, United Kingdom

Frequent flyer miles and book promotion led to free travel, meals, and two nights' accommodation in Worthing on the South Coast of England. It was October 1990 and we were guest speakers at a weekend conference of the Restricted Growth Association, the English equivalent of LPA. We rented a car because we planned on sightseeing for a week after the conference. After the debacle at the NZ car rental agency, we pre-paid for this car and did not give advance notice of our stature. This was not a deception, but rather timing the disclosure to coincide with our arrival at the service desk. We were counting on the difficulty of refusing service to someone standing there with a pre-paid voucher for a reserved car.

At Heathrow airport, we waited at the designated place for a ride to the car rental agency. Still, the airport driver for the rental company told us we were in the wrong line. We assured him that we were in the right line because we were renting a car. He loaded our bags into his van with obvious skepticism and waited to see what would happen at the service desk. When we presented our voucher, the young clerk disappeared behind closed doors. A more senior person eventually emerged and asked how we planned to drive the car.

Robert showed him our pedal extensions and seat cushions. Despite their doubts, management reluctantly agreed to let Robert install the extensions. To our chagrin, the brake pedal extension would not fit. Word of our presence had spread like wildfire and Robert artfully transformed this curious audience into a team of helpers. The agency mechanics became just as determined as Robert to attach the pedal extensions safely. The company ended up bringing in another car with a different brake pedal design, while Robert met probably every mechanic on the lot before the extensions were successfully installed two hours later.

Then it was my turn. The manager insisted on driving around the block with us to be sure that we were not an insurance risk. Robert appointed me to drive since I grew up driving on the left side of the road in New Zealand, even though I was sleep-deprived having traveled through the night. Also, the block was a busy London road that fed into a three-lane traffic circle. It was a relief to pass the driving test and finally be on our way.

We had an ambitious itinerary that included Salisbury Cathedral, Stonehenge, Bath, Stratford-on-Avon, the Lake District, and London. Most of our accommodations were in bed-and- breakfast private homes. We felt the access challenges were worth it to soak in more British culture and cuisine. Did it really matter that we had to leave our bedroom door ajar because we could not reach the door handle?

We spent more time at Salisbury Cathedral, built in 1220, than at Stonehenge which is anywhere from 3,500 to 5,000 years old. The rock formations were impressive, but we preferred the cathedral planned in the shape of a cross and the 404-foot spire designed to lift our thoughts upwards to God. It was a privilege to lay eyes on one of the four surviving original texts of the 1215 Magna Carta preserving the right to a fair trial and a free church.

In Bath, we saw the Roman influence in England in AD 75. Here they built baths in the only mineral hot springs in the country. Robert handled the modern-day parking problem in the historic section of town by flagging down an officer who put a sign in our car window: *Driver and passenger are both disabled from U.S.A. but do not have disabled badge.* Tickets avoided.

We missed seeing a Shakespearian play in Stratford-on-Avon because we were in town between plays. At least we saw Shakespeare's birthplace and Ann Hathaway's cottage. Our literary tour continued in the Lake

District where we saw Dove Cottage, one of William Wordsworth's homes, and the countryside that inspired much of his writing.

We packed our 36 hours in London with a Thames River ride that gave us a view of Parliament buildings, Big Ben, St. Paul's Cathedral, Greenwich Village, and the Tower of London. We saw Buckingham Palace and a musical matinee, *Return to the Forbidden Planet*. We dined with my Aunt Susan who had lived in England for 17 years. We left England with a strong taste for a return visit one day.

New York Weekends in Adirondacks and Mexico

We celebrated our sixth wedding anniversary with a fall 1987 weekend in the New York Adirondacks—a rare treat taking time out for just the two of us. The trees were a spectacular gold, yellow, red, and orange. We enhanced our view on the ski lift to the top of McCauley Mountain and in a motorboat ride in the Fulton Chain of Lakes.

In August 1990, we went camping with the New York Finger Lakes LPA Chapter in Mexico, New York. We chose a campsite with no electricity so we could enjoy the river meandering past our tent. However, we arrived after dark without a lantern and needed help putting up the tent. We were late because Robert's idea of being ready to leave when I got home from work was having a borrowed kayak strapped on top of the van. He had not packed any food, bedding, or camping gear.

Despite the rough start, we still had a good time. Robert had his kayak and rubber raft in the river and I sat in my sun chair at the river's edge reading and watching him and the other chapter members splashing around. My pleasure was somewhat muted because my reading material was for the August 17th Multistate Professional Responsibility Exam—an ethics exam—which is administered separately from the New York bar exam. Thankfully, this one was only two hours unlike the two-day bar exam.

New Zealand Friends in Rochester

Also that summer, we enjoyed a four-day visit from my NZ law school friends—Packiam, John, and their two children, Ashwind and Divia. I was disappointed that my study for the ethics exam took away some of our time together. On our way to Niagara Falls, we even detoured in Buffalo for me to take the exam.

Chapter 11
Prayer and Protection

Health Challenges

At age 42, Robert had the first of four eye surgeries: two to remove cataracts and two to implant the intraocular lens. The cataract and lens implants were done five years apart because the surgeon did not want the artificial lens to obstruct access to Robert's retina. Access was important because retinal detachment is a risk for Robert due to having SED. In the meantime, Robert was content with successful removal of the cataracts, as he could continue wearing contacts—without which he was legally blind in his right eye.

At age 36, I had severe pain and immobility in my left shoulder. I'd had it before, but this time, rest and over-the-counter medication didn't solve the problem. I was skeptical when the orthopedist referred me to physical therapy. Thankfully, after three months of anti-inflammatory pills, heating pads, ultrasound, stretching, and exercise, I was pain-free and had improved range of motion.

Soon afterwards, Robert had outpatient hernia surgery. I was grateful our house cleaners were still at the house when we got home from the hospital. Robert definitely needed a stronger arm than mine to lean on to get from the car to the bedroom. My careful attention to the doctor's instructions did him more harm than good. The doctor had prescribed codeine tablets every four hours. I even woke Robert up during the night to keep the four-hour schedule. But after about 36 hours, Robert was more nauseous than when he first came home from the hospital. Finally, he was alert enough to ask me what medication he was taking. When I said codeine, he remembered that codeine makes him sick. The doctor agreed that he could discontinue the codeine and substitute over-the-counter medication for the pain. After the pain subsided, Robert struggled with his two-week driving restriction. I was extremely thankful for his niece Juliette spending Thanksgiving week with us; she was able to alleviate Robert's boredom by playing cards with him.

Bible Study and Prayer Impact

My Fall 1989 ladies Bible study in 1 Corinthians convicted me to address the issue of my temper. I did not know I had such a bad temper—

until I got married. Robert was a master at pressing all my buttons. Yet I needed to apply biblical truth:

> *No temptation has overtaken you but such as is common to man; and God is faithful, who will not allow you to be tempted beyond what you are able, but with the temptation will provide the way of escape also, so that you will be able to endure it.* ∞ *1 Corinthians 10:13*

I also needed to take to heart the biblical lessons of love:

> *Love is patient, love . . . does not act unbecomingly; it does not seek its own, is not provoked, does not take into account a wrong suffered.* ∞ *1 Corinthians 13:4-5*

I prayed for these qualities because I was too easily offended and vocal about Robert's conduct.

My ongoing prayers for Robert's spiritual state saw an answer in November 1989 when he attended a Sunday school class with me to study the book, *Love is a Decision*.[1] It was Robert's first time coming to Sunday school, the first time we had formally worked on our relationship, and our first step to understanding what it takes to have a healthy marriage. We saw how we needed to change, but it was years before we consistently honored and nurtured one another and responded biblically to high stress situations.

The class had one immediate effect. It inspired Robert to give me flowers for the first time. Before then, he was unwilling to buy me cut flowers because he hated to watch them die in the vase. After the class, he was willing to give me a bouquet of roses knowing how much I would enjoy them. I was touched to see him put my interests before his own.

After we finished the marriage class, Robert did not become a regular at Sunday school, despite my prayers. However, he did enjoy a men's retreat and volunteered at the Flower City work camp during Easter of 1990. He could not do construction work on the inner-city homes selected for repairs, but he could use his computer skills to organize the materials and tools needed for each job site. I was happy when he agreed to join me at a church home fellowship group in the summer of 1990.

In one of our home fellowship studies, we took a burnout assessment inventory. My score indicated I was experiencing moderate burnout and should do something about it. I decided after six years working at Lawyers Cooperative Publishing (LCP) it was time to change jobs. After I was sworn in as a member of the New York State bar in January 1991,

I mailed my resume to several law firms and prayed for a good outcome. Despite some positive feedback on my credentials, most firms had no openings and did not offer an interview. The couple of interviews I landed did not result in a job offer. Even a feature article in the *Rochester Business Magazine* did not lead to a job opportunity.

Nonetheless, God heard my prayers. He gave me the desired job change without the need to change employers. The July 26, 1990 passage of the Americans with Disabilities Act (ADA)—a civil rights law for people with disabilities—presented an opportunity for a new publication. LCP accepted my proposal to publish a four-binder set called the *Americans with Disabilities: Practice and Compliance Manual* covering the ADA and several other disability civil rights laws. Initially, I shared responsibility for planning, writing and editing chapters included in the manual. The assignment soon earned me a promotion to senior editor with full charge of the project. I enjoyed the extra responsibility, especially the interaction with marketing and sales staff. LCP enjoyed the initial sales far exceeding their expectations.

A State of Emergency

God's protection was again evident after the declaration of a state of emergency in Rochester on March 4, 1991, when an inch of solid ice enveloped the city. Twelve-hundred telephone poles were down; more than half the city's homes lost electricity; tree limbs fractured; and travel came to a standstill. It was called the worst ice storm in almost 100 years.

During the night we thought there was a thunderstorm and mistook a tree branch falling on our garage roof for a thunderclap. When the alarm went off, Robert dragged himself out of bed and into the shower. He happily came back to bed when I told him it was only 3:00 a.m. We were too tired to answer the phone ringing off the hook at 5:30 a.m., but when the doorbell rang at 6:00 a.m., we knew something was wrong. It was a firefighter warning us not to go outside because of all the fallen branches and live wires dancing on the ground. Robert immediately got dressed and went outside to see for himself. Mr. Curiosity at work.

Despite the ice and debris everywhere, it was beautiful. Glistening silver covered the trees set against a clear blue sky. Robert, and thousands like him, got some spectacular photos. Camera film was among the shortages named in the two-week recovery period after the storm. The loss of almost half the city's trees was well documented.

Adaptive Living Marketing

Robert's professional and personal accomplishments were also well documented in 1991. A chapter about Robert, "Problem Solving from a Different Perspective," was published in a book titled, *The Challenged Scientists: Disabilities and the Triumph of Excellence*.[3] Robert had agreed to be interviewed hoping that the book's influence would help advance Adaptive Living.

In the same year, Robert tried very hard to promote Adaptive Living by extending his sphere of influence with service on several committees, including appointments from New York State Governor Mario Cuomo and Rochester Mayor Thomas P. Ryan, Jr. On the national front, in 1992 Robert's colleagues elected him to a three-year term as a board member of the Rehabilitation Engineering Society of North America (RESNA).

While Robert basked in this recognition, I asked him, "Which committee are you going to give up?"

It was clear to me that all his committee work would leave very little time to generate revenue.

Chapter 12
Seeing the Light of Day

Marriage Troubles

Flying from Rochester, New York, to Washington, DC, sporting new diamonds and rubies next to my wedding band was a good start to our tenth-anniversary weekend. Robert expressed his love well with this ring, roses and very meaningful words in his anniversary card to me:

> *It's been 10 marvelous years having you at my side in the good times and the difficult ones . . . growing and learning, finding out more about each other, understanding our sensitive qualities, . . . we have grown stronger and closer to Christ. . . . Angela, you've made a positive change in my life. I look forward to the next 10 years together and the challenges they bring.*

We relived our first "date" to the Lincoln Memorial, including the part about getting lost on the way, which—after 10 years of getting lost with Robert—I no longer found amusing. His loving words on the anniversary card were soon lost on me. The weekend came to a sorry end when Robert could not find where to return the rental car at the airport and underestimated how long it would take to remove the pedal extensions. I was furious and stormed off to the departure gate without him. I boarded without him too, but he made it to his seat next to me before the plane took off.

This tempest occurred one week before a church marriage enrichment weekend that I was helping to plan as a member of the family life committee. Clearly, I was more suited for the role of guest than wedding planner. Friday night was a wedding reception with guests invited to wear something from their wedding day. Robert and I were among several people who could still fit their full bridal regalia; others wore a veil, gloves, or a cummerbund. Our attire, a guest book, gifts, speeches, a wedding cake, photos, food, and entertainment prepared us well for Sandy and Margie Mason's teaching on how to have a healthy marriage. Robert and I needed all the help we could get.

Adaptive Living Moved Out of the Basement

Robert's business was a huge stressor on our relationship. In November 1991, Adaptive Living saw the light of day when it moved out of our home basement into a commercial office building in the Erie Canal district. Robert saw a future in buying the property because it was close to downtown Rochester and Kodak's world headquarters. The purchase was only possible because God graciously responded to the prayers from our church friends with the following answers:

- The Small Business Administration (SBA) loan program was funded the year of Robert's application.
- Robert was the first Rochester business owner in two years to qualify for the SBA loan for people with disabilities.
- The SBA commercial loan interest rate was 3% compared to bank rates of 16% and the SBA mortgage term was 20 years compared to bank terms of 10-15 years.
- Robert was approved at an affordable price for the life insurance policy required by the SBA; this had been a concern due to Robert's dwarfism and lack of data on life expectancy for those with his type of dwarfism.
- Renovation funds were part of the SBA loan and matched by a City of Rochester community-development grant allowing for building improvements.
- The city cleaned up neighborhood debris, demolished a derelict building, and added a fence behind the property.

All was well until I learned that the SBA loan required me to sign as guarantor and use our home as collateral. I was distraught. If the business failed, my salary could not cover two mortgages and we could lose our house. For me it was a deal breaker. For Robert, not to do so was a marriage breaker. Amidst my tears and protest, Robert promised me that if the business could not pay, he would get another job to pay the loan. And so, I signed the loan papers with extreme reluctance.

The intent of moving the business was not only for Adaptive Living to grow and be physically more accessible to clients, but also for Robert to be more accessible to me. He worked day and night in his home office and agreed to come home from his new office each evening before dark. I believed him because the neighborhood was not safe after dark.

New Year Growling

Some of that promised together time happened when we rang in the 1992 New Year with Robert's family in Florida. One of the highlights was on Big Pine Key with David Buerkle and his sons, James and John, when we stopped to see Key deer. Instead, we saw children throwing stones into a pond while asking, "Is it real, is it real?"

Their target was a submerged seven-foot, battle-scarred alligator. Robert did not know if the gator was real, but he did not need stones to find out. We were enthralled when Robert did a gator growl, a low vibrating guttural sound. What happened next stunned us all.

The gator rose to the surface and locked eyes on Robert. It was definitely real. In an instant, the gator could have run onto the observation deck where we stood above him. David was ready to run with a son under each arm and Robert and I appeared to be on the menu for the gator's next meal. However, Robert convinced us all to freeze in place. Thankfully, the gator saw no threat and sank back to the bottom of the pond. It was time to get out of there, swiftly. As we hurried away, we overheard more kids throwing stones at the gator and asking if it was real. We hoped none of them knew the gator growl.

We were not anxious to return to the Rochester winter at the end of the vacation. That's when I took to growling. It was no gator growl, rather a complaint about Robert's broken promise to work regular hours. Robert actually worked more hours to cover the increased overhead, maintain the building, and form a neighborhood business association to address graffiti and crime problems.

It did not help that our bird Budgie died in February. Deciding on his burial caused one more conflict. Robert wanted to put Budgie in the garbage since we could not bury him in the frozen ground. I wanted to put Budgie in the freezer until the spring thaw when we could bury him in the yard with a grave marker. I prevailed for a week, but Robert could not cope with opening the freezer knowing Budgie was in there. So, Budgie found his final resting place somewhere in Rochester's refuse pile.

Travel Diversions

Robert was too busy to join me on a NZ trip where I was the keynote speaker at the annual conference for CCS,[1] a nationwide organization that provides support, advocacy, and information for people with disabilities. The trip was a welcome diversion from marriage and business struggles. In addition to delivering the keynote speech on disability rights, I was the subject of a media blitz with 14 interviews in only four days. After the conference, there were 5 more media interviews in Australia due to a press release on *Dwarfs Don't Live in Doll Houses*. Thankfully, I still had time to enjoy visiting family and friends.

On my return from Sydney, Australia, I stopped in San Francisco for a few days at the 1992 LPA national conference. Robert was already there and after being apart for three weeks, I expected a warm welcome. Instead, I could not find him for several hours. He had lost track of time while helping a friend repair a flat tire on her wheelchair. Despite his admirable cause, this left me totally deflated.

I was not the only one upset with Robert that week. A motorcycle cop pulled him over as we drove to Fisherman's Wharf with two little people NZ delegates: Carolyn Wilcock and Raewyn Fridd. Robert had stopped the car on the highway in the yellow-striped V between two lanes that forked in different directions. There was no need for my backseat commentary—the cop took the words right out of my mouth. The day was memorable, especially since a photo of the four of us at Fisherman's Wharf was on the LPA brochure for many years.

Marriage Counseling

On the home front, I was totally exasperated with Robert's 90-plus hour work weeks. I was alone on nights and weekends and had to negotiate to get Robert to do anything with me. His only concession was to come to church on Sunday morning and a home fellowship every other week. I tried everything to get Robert to come home from work at a reasonable hour: helping with his work, bribing him with food, calling to remind him of the time, demanding an apology when he came home late, screaming at him when he acted like nothing was wrong, writing him letters pouring out my distress, sleeping on the couch, and lots of crying. It was the worst of two worlds—the loneliness of being single with the constraints of being married.

Finally, one night in March of 1993, I was so desperate I made an appointment for marriage counseling with John Lohman, our church Pastor of Family Life and Counseling. It was good that Robert agreed to come with me because I was very close to walking out on him. Initially, Pastor John saw a simple communication problem that could be resolved in a couple of sessions. However, a closer look revealed deep-seated, unresolved issues that led to 12 counseling sessions over six months.

The counseling showed that Robert was a workaholic entering the late stages on the Work Addiction Scale. And I was codependent. Robert had ulcers and emotional deadness. According to my reading of the scale, he was only two steps away from death. Robert had long surpassed the early stage of constantly thinking of work, not taking any days off, and consistently exceeding a 40-hour workweek. His almost nonexistent social life, giving up on relationship obligations, and failed attempts to change showed he had definitely passed the middle stage.

Pastor John helped us understand the dynamics of our relationship by taking a family history and having us do the Minnesota Multiphasic Personality Inventory. The results showed that we both had a lot of work to do as individuals and as a couple. We started with a renewal of our marriage vows. We also took the word divorce off the table, especially in the middle of an argument.

For several months, we worked on our relationship vision, childhood frustrations, a partner profile, unfinished business, and communication. We even wrote pledges to each other on issues relating to responsibilities, scheduling, spending time together, and supporting one another. We finally were seeing the light of day in our marriage.

Chapter 13
Family Highs and Business Low

My One and Only American Football Game

Robert's brothers—Mickey and Peter—came from Florida for a Miami Dolphins and Buffalo Bills game in Buffalo, New York. The brothers had even arranged for us to stay at the same hotel as the Dolphins the night before the game. Their first objective—to see Dolphins up close—was achieved when we squeezed into the same elevator. I even touched a Dolphin in a defensive move to stop him from standing on me. I had no idea who he was, but accepted the apology of Dolphin #80 along with his illegible autograph.

We scored a second goal when we got the autograph of Dolphin #91. After dinner, Mickey tilted the odds in our favor by taking us back to the floor where the Dolphins had exited the elevator earlier. We casually ran into this player at the soda machine, and he not only posed for a photograph with us, but we posed with him for a photograph on his camera.

Above all else, the brothers were ecstatic when the Dolphins beat the Bills the next day. My pleasure was that my one and only American football game finally ended. It was no fun walking miles to our seats, and even being carried up half the steep stairs—knowing I could not drink anything for hours lest it prompt a need to go to the bathroom. Worst of all, I was not properly dressed for outdoor seating in the freezing rain that was so cold Peter's moustache froze. To cap it off, I missed the action when everyone roared and leaped to their feet.

Unexpected Holiday Excitement

Our Thanksgiving week in 1993 was more exciting than usual. The doorbell rang just before midnight. It was a surprise to receive a visitor at this late hour and quite extraordinary for the visitor to be from the Rochester Police Department. On this cold and rainy night, snow was not the only threat.

Earlier in the evening, a cab had dropped Juliette off to spend the holiday with us. She was alarmed to find the house in darkness, no cars in the garage, no answer to the doorbell, and no key to get in.

In desperation she walked to the corner store and called her mother in Florida: "I'm locked out of the house and there's nothing for me to do but walk the streets of Rochester and OOOOH it's SOOOOO cold and wet."

When Paula could not get us on the phone, she called the police. Meanwhile, Robert came home before Juliette had walked one block back to the house. Clearly, the attempt to call off the police alert had failed.

On December 24th, my sister, Deborah, was home in Sydney, Australia, ready to celebrate her birthday with Robert and me. But instead of being locked out of the house, Robert was blocked from boarding the plane in Los Angeles. His passport was current, but this time he was missing an Australian visa. We were held over one day while Robert got his visa at the Australian Consulate's office, arriving just before the office closed early for the Christmas break. I was frustrated to miss Deborah's birthday, but at least we arrived in time to celebrate Christmas together for the first time in seven years.

Our family time was great, especially holding Samuel, the three-month-old son of my brother, Greg. We enjoyed talking, going to the beach, having barbecues, shopping and sightseeing. Robert especially enjoyed swimming, fishing, and photographing the kids on the trampoline.

Robert's wheelchair was a great attraction to the kids and the cause of one bone-chilling moment. My niece Nadia had raced the wheelchair along the balcony, gone full flight off the end, and crashed onto the driveway one story below. It was miraculous she suffered no injuries; with her dancing skills, Nadia instinctively separated herself from the wheelchair mid-flight and avoided landing on her head.

In New Zealand, we spent most of our time relaxing with relatives and friends. Fishing with Dutch, a family friend, was Robert's highlight, even when Robert became the catch of the day in the Weymouth estuary. Dad fished Robert out of the mud into which he sank when following a flock of ducks. Robert redeemed himself with Dad when he caught enough flounder to provide dinner for the family and our extra visitors.

Asheville and Everglades

In May 1994, we spent time with the Buerkle family, first at Juliette's graduation from St. Bonaventure University and then on vacation in Asheville, North Carolina. We broke the 12-hour drive from Rochester in half so that we could enjoy some sights along the way. The New River Gorge in West Virginia could have been Robert's undoing. After safely winding our way down the narrow mountain road to the bottom of the gorge, Robert ignored the *Bridge Closed* sign to get closer to some local boys who were bungee jumping off the bridge. I was not amused when Robert walked onto the bridge with gaping holes in the wooden planks and seriously considered making his own bungee jump.

Our time in Asheville was lovely as we stayed in the Essers' cabin set remotely in the wooded hill country. Robert's nephews James and John were great companions for testing Robert's new tent and going fishing. I was more interested in visiting the Biltmore 250-room mansion with Paula and Juliette. Robert and I both enjoyed the scenic highway of the Great Smoky Mountains National Park.

In January 1995, Robert was welcomed to the Florida Everglades National Park with a random sign on the side of the road: *Robert is Here*. We shared our adventure with the Buerkle and Chafin families. Juliette, the men, and the boys set up tents in the camping ground with a spectacular ocean view of Florida Bay. Paula, Susan, and I set up in a cottage, trading the view for air conditioning, a bathroom, and kitchenette. Most of all, I was glad to escape the mosquitoes and biting flies. Even though the campers laughed at the three women opting for comfort, they did not hesitate to visit our cottage for food and amenities.

Robert accepted that swimming was inadvisable due to four poisonous snakes—diamondback and pygmy rattlesnakes, coral snakes, and water moccasins—making the Everglades their home. However, he ignored the if-you-don't-bother-them-they-won't-bother-you advice when confronted by a growling alligator. When the canoe he shared with Juliette and her friend unexpectedly disturbed an alligator resting on an embankment, Robert tried to convince them not to paddle away until he got a photo. They had the sense not to listen to him.

Embezzled

After a revolving door of secretaries, Robert hired Secretary #7 in September 1993. He was confident she would do well with her bright personality, four-year degree, and work experience. Besides, we had known her since she was a teenager. What we didn't know was that as soon as she learned how to operate the accounting program, she also learned how to divert funds to herself. After only six weeks of employment, she embezzled the first of 21 checks. We knew money was tight, but didn't make the connection until after she was fired in April 1994 for poor performance, unpredictable behavior, and lying.

After Secretary #7's termination, Robert noticed some bookkeeping anomalies and requested copies of canceled checks from the bank. We were stunned to see Robert's forged signature for checks paid to herself or directly to one of her creditors. She even forged a check to pay her taxes.

Secretary #7 was arrested, charged with 21 felony counts of forgery and altering business records. She had embezzled $9,164.68. Although she could have served prison time, a plea bargain led to three years' probation, counseling, and restitution. Her father was a big part of this generous deal because his restitution payment of $4,000 to the court persuaded the district attorney to plead the charges down to misdemeanors. The reason Secretary #7 gave for stealing? She needed the money. We did not want her to go to prison, but in his victim statement to the judge, Robert recommended community service hoping it would give her an appreciation of those truly in need. She never apologized for her actions, but we were amazed when she did pay all the court-ordered restitution. The bank manager told us that this almost never happens.

Although business was still a challenge, Robert was happy to hire a part-time secretary, on September 11, 1994. Lynette was a Pastor's wife and had the Christian character that Secretary #7 lacked.

Spiritual Growth

Our church home fellowship group stood with us in prayer and support during the embezzlement ordeal. It was a time of spiritual growth culminating in our baptism by full immersion on April 24, 1994. The whole event would have been underwater if a retired carpenter had not built a special platform for us to stand on in the baptismal until the appropriate moment. Before the baptism, we each gave our testimony of God's grace, love, and faithfulness in our lives. The baptism was a public profession of our faith and belief in Jesus Christ as our Lord and Savior.

Chapter 14
What a Difference Ten Years Makes

Our Work Status

March 1995 marked the ten-year anniversary of Adaptive Living. The local newspaper reported the milestone and clearly described Adaptive Living services, Robert's credentials, and his perspective on how technology improvements in the last decade benefited people with disabilities. The article also expressed Robert's budget and marketing worries that made it difficult for him to reach the people who needed his services.[1] Despite his concerns, Robert persevered with the business and continued contributing to the community with his professional and volunteer services.[2]

After 10 years with LCP, I was promoted to project editor. I still managed the Americans with Disabilities publication series[3] with planning, coordinating contractors, editing, training, writing and marketing input.

Maturing in our Christian Walk

West Side Baptist had been our home church for six years. Here we found preaching that was clear, relevant, and biblical that helped us grow and mature in our Christian walk. We both responded in ministry service: Robert taught third-grade Sunday school and I taught some women's Bible studies. I served as a librarian on a monthly rotation and began a two-year term on the Christian education board.

Our home fellowship group was our best opportunity to minister to individual needs. We met every other week to eat, pray, laugh, and learn together. We kept a prayer journal so that we would remember to pray for specific needs and especially to praise God for His interventions. In the summer, we hosted a vacation party where people brought food that they like to eat on vacation and a few pictures for a slideshow of our favorite vacations.

We helped to plan a church talent show followed by an ice-cream social. Robert brought the house down with his comedy debut in a skit he planned and performed with four other people.

The women's winter Bible study on contentment was well-timed. The studies on being content—with self, in stress, in trials, in relationships, in physical afflictions, and with little or much—were all good preparation for future challenges. For example, both of our careers were uncertain in 1996. Adaptive Living was not doing well. Although my employer LCP was doing well, a corporate merger resulted in many job losses and staff transfers.[4] It was not known whether my job would be eliminated or relocated to Eagan, Minnesota. We persevered and trusted God for His next move.

In the spring, I prepared a Bible study on joy for our home fellowship group. I went beyond what the 15-minute devotional required and, for my own benefit, did a complete word study. It was good to be reminded that the Triune God—Father, Son, and Holy Spirit—is the source of our joy from which we gain strength. We can express and experience joy when we respond to God's character and actions on our behalf.

> *The LORD is my strength and my shield;*
> *my heart trusts in Him, and I am helped;*
> *Therefore my heart exults,*
> *and with my song I shall thank Him.* ∞ *Psalm 28:7*

Our marriage relationship was a work in progress. In the fall of 1995, we signed up for the Sunday school class studying the book, *Fit to Be Tied.*[5] The early chapters on marriage preparation were quite frustrating because they highlighted the areas in which we had fallen short. The chapters on marriage conflict, understanding our differences, and improving our communication were helpful.

In June 1996, Robert was uplifted at a Promise Keepers conference in Syracuse, New York. The speakers were dynamic, but singing with about 40,000 men was the highlight. This conference motivated Robert to accept the fourth-grade Sunday school teaching assignment. I can also say that he became more responsive to my needs as his wife.

In October and November, I led the Tuesday evening women's Bible study on the book of James. It was a challenging study encouraging Christians to mature in their faith through perseverance in trials, hear and respond to God's Word, control their tongue, seek godly wisdom, and develop patience.

Sliced Open like a Can

Robert did very well communicating a crisis when he called me at work one morning saying, "I've had an accident, but I'm okay." I believed him since he—rather than an emergency worker—was the one making the call.

Robert had been driving on a suburban street when he suddenly heard glass popping and saw the passenger side of his van sliced open like a can. The thin metal edge of the flatbed truck in the adjacent lane jutted into Robert's lane and cut through his van. The truck driver, preparing to make a sharp turn, had moved the rear wheels forward causing the back of the truck to swing wide and hide the brake and turn signal lights. Robert escaped unscathed, but the van was totaled.

The insurance company paid Robert for a replacement vehicle. However, Snappy Car Rentals refused to allow Robert to use his pedal extensions on their vehicle and would only allow him to use hand controls. We did not have the time or energy to pursue this violation of the ADA. Instead, another car rental company profited from Robert's business.

More Camping and Water Sports

We rang in the New Year of 1996 camping at Myall Lakes in New South Wales, Australia. Unlike the Everglades, we both slept in a tent. We joined Deborah and Rob, Nadia and Ashley, and their friends. The lakes were beautiful and our campsite had electricity, a refrigerator, and an awning off the side of a bus covering tables and chairs.

It was a very relaxing few days with the exception of the scariest three hours in Robert's life. His joyride on a Jet Ski turned into terror when he got lost on his way back to the camping ground. He tried a shortcut across the lake, but it was so cold and choppy that he went

Deborah sets us up for jet ski ride

numb and his joints hurt from cutting through the waves. Robert knew he wasn't going to make it this way, so he went back to the shoreline. However, the weeds clogged up the Jet Ski, twice. Asking people for directions was of no help because Robert forgot the name of our camping ground—one of many around the lakes. He finally returned, worse for the wear. Once he recovered, he was most upset to have missed seeing a huge goanna lizard take a leisurely stroll through our camping ground.

After Myall Lakes, we drove south to camp with Greg and Julie, Holly, and Samuel at Kiama, New South Wales. We started in a two-person tent, but moved into the family tent when ours got soaked. The rain changed our outdoor plans, but the tree frogs had a blast. Greg's attempt to quiet them down at night by yelling and throwing cans was futile, albeit entertaining to watch. We amused ourselves reading out loud and discussing *Men are from Mars, Women are from Venus,*[6] shopping, going to the movies, reading, and playing cards. The weather cooperated enough for us to visit a wildlife park where we walked among the kangaroos, hand-feeding them with food bought at the park.

When we returned to Sydney, Robert and Ray—a groomsman at our NZ wedding—made a day of fishing at Bradley's Head, a peninsula overlooking Sydney Harbor south of the Mosman district. Four years later, Tom Cruise landed at this jetty to rescue a female hostage in a scene from the film *Mission Impossible 2*. Robert and Ray's assignment was to stay clear of the killer toxin in the pufferfish they caught. There is no known antidote.

On our return to the US, we stopped at the Naviti Resort on the Coral Coast of Viti Levu, Fiji. We needed some couple time and it helped me recover emotionally from separating from my family. For two nights and three days we enjoyed the relaxed culture that Fiji has to offer, especially the tropical fruit, the friendly indigenous people, and viewing the colorful fish from the glass-bottom boat. It truly is paradise.

Robert found a snorkeling buddy and got much more than he bargained for. Only two hours before our departure to the airport, Robert stood dripping blood on the beachfront restaurant verandah. Robert was reaching for a dark blue starfish when an electric eel engraved its teeth marks across his second and third fingers. Medical attention was needed.

The good news was that the doctor on call was at the hotel; the bad news was that the doctor was in the bar having a few drinks. We reluctantly went with the doctor to his off-site clinic, but only because another staff member was the designated driver. Robert accepted a tetanus shot, but declined sutures. This was a good decision because the doctor's impaired state made him clumsy and sloppy. By the time we got to Nadi airport, the doctor's bandage was falling off.

When I came out of the airport bathroom, I could not find Robert. However, I suspected that he might have something to do with the crowd near the terminal entrance. I was right. Robert was at the center of the throng, accommodating parent requests for children to have their photograph taken with him. We don't know if they thought he was a celebrity or a good luck charm. Whatever the attraction, I rescued Robert and we went to the pre-boarding lounge. Here Robert connected with two passengers—an American EMT and a mother traveling the world with two young children. Together they had the skill and supplies to properly bandage Robert's wound.

In September, Robert spent a get-away fishing weekend in Thousand Islands, New York with three other men from church. All four were avid fishermen, which, in my opinion, means they don't look at their watches or wonder how much longer before heading back to land.

Chapter 15

For Shorter or Taller, Closer or Farther

First Hip Replacement

It had been more than a year since Robert had any surgery, but he was clearly in physical distress. I knew this—because lately I no longer needed an alarm clock to wake up in the mornings—because the sound of Robert's crutches clip-clopping around the house was my alarm. Regrettably, I could not set this alarm for when I was ready to get up.

Robert's hip pain—so bad it woke him at night and made walking difficult during the day—was due to joint deterioration and hairline fractures in both hips. He maintained his mobility with four pairs of crutches: one for my car, one for his van, one for the house, and one for the office. Hip replacement surgery was imminent.

We were pleased to have health insurance that covered out-of-state surgery at the Cleveland Clinic in Ohio. Robert had confidence in Dr. Mary Matejczyk, an orthopedist and surgeon at that clinic where she specialized in both hip replacements and dwarfism. We found no such specialist in Rochester, New York, so we scheduled the first surgery in Cleveland on April 30, 1997, and planned for the second to follow three months later.

It was a shock when my employer eliminated our health plan on March 31st. Although we could switch to an HMO, such plans rarely approve out-of-state surgeries. As a result, we rescheduled the first surgery for February 24th, but did not know what to do about the second surgery. Our home fellowship group offered to do the surgery on the dining room table, but they also prayed with us for a better plan.

In desperation, I wrote to my employer's senior vice president asking for reconsideration of the health plan decision. The company did not change its mind, but they did connect me with the benefits specialist in human resources. Together we persuaded the HMO that the second out-of-state surgery was medically necessary. This was a huge relief and answer to prayer.

In January 1997, Robert prepared himself for his surgery ordeal by snorkeling with a school of barracudas at the John Pennekamp Coral Reef State Park in Key Largo, Florida. Thankfully, Robert did not look like a menu item. The plan had been to swim among fish common to the reef, but a Cheez Whiz squirt bottle was needed to attract the beautiful fish and not the barracudas.

Finding the underwater Christ of the Abyss statue made snorkeling the second day a complete success. In 25 feet of water, the 16-foot statue is magnificent with Jesus's arms reaching out to embrace the beauty of His creation. This image was a great encouragement to Robert as he geared up for the surgery to replace his left hip.

Robert did what he could to make the surgery go smoothly, including self-donating two units of blood. He also shared a medical article on anesthesia and dwarfism with the chief of anesthesiology. On the day of surgery, he refused any anesthetic until the assigned anesthesiologist assured him she had read the article. My comfort was in Scripture:

Now I know that the LORD saves His anointed;
He will answer him from His holy heaven
with the saving strength of His right hand.
Some boast in chariots and some in horses,
But we will boast in the name of the LORD, our God.
∞ Psalm 20:6-7

Dr. Matejczyk described the two-and-a-half-hour surgery as rigorous, but said it went well. She used 36 staples to close the incision. Tanked up on three pints of blood and morphine, Robert was high as a kite when he was wheeled into his room after the surgery. He repeatedly shared God's blessing with the transporter and greeted me with enthusiasm. I choked up seeing him hooked up to tubes and oxygen.

Bob and Margaret, friends from when we lived in Cleveland, gave me a six-day oasis during Robert's hospital stay. I relaxed with them in the mornings, visited Robert at the hospital from noon until 8:00 p.m., and then returned to unwind from the day. Robert had many visitors from our years living in Cleveland and received many get-well cards. The hand-made cards from his Sunday School students had colorful drawings and Bible verse references. The children said they were all praying for Robert and looking forward to him coming back to teach. As one child wrote, *I hope your surgery gose well. God is with you alwas.*

On day three after the surgery, a disheveled, unshaven Robert on his way to his first physical therapy session asked me, "How do I look?"

I answered, "Wonderful. You look better and better every day."

A single male nurse overheard the conversation and said, "Every man should have a wife like you."

Needless to say, I remind Robert of this on a regular basis.

Robert worked hard in therapy—twice on weekdays and once on weekend days. His discharge from the hospital to home depended on him being able to climb stairs. He was so determined to achieve this goal that the therapist observed that he must be a workaholic.

When the social worker was making discharge plans that included in-home physical therapy, Robert asked, "When can I go back to work?"

Somewhat startled, she replied, "We don't believe in insurance fraud here." In other words, qualifying for in-home services is synonymous with not being physically able to leave the house, not even for work.

The social worker asked me about arrangements for airlifting Robert from Cleveland to Rochester. She was surprised to learn that our transport plan was for Robert to recline on the back seat of our Honda wagon with multiple pillows, a water bottle, urinal, and reading material. Hospital staff helped him into the vehicle in Cleveland and home fellowship members helped him out in Rochester. After all, it was only a five-hour drive of about 250 miles.

Our home fellowship group also set Robert up at home. Jim and Chuck installed bathroom accommodations—a handgrip, support rails, and a platform around the toilet so that his legs would not dangle. Mary and Melody brought us a meal. Gary and Chuck set up the computer. Once he recovered from the shock of a two-week house arrest, Robert made good use of the computer, working at home and doing our taxes online between therapy and nurse visits.

Within a week of being home from the hospital, we received one of those calls you never want to get. At 3:00 a.m. Robert's brother Peter called to tell us that Daniel Van Etten, their 19-year-old nephew, had died in a car accident in Georgia. Daniel was the only son of Mickey and Kim and brother of Veronica. He was a freshman lineman on a football scholarship at West Virginia University. Words cannot express the heartache caused by his death. In Daniel's memory, the 1997 Mountaineers team at West Virginia University wore his initials on their helmets. The University also established a scholarship in Daniel's name. The family will always remember Daniel as a *true Van Etten*; one who walked in his grandfather's footsteps as a great fisherman and athlete.

Daniel's death was a terrible loss made especially difficult because Robert could not travel to the funeral. We made a special trip in July to spend a few days with Mickey and Kim.

Second Hip Replacement

In June 1997, Robert prepared himself for his second surgery ordeal by attending Camp Victory, an LPA District 2 weekend in Millville, Pennsylvania. We enjoyed community meals and activities without the rough-it drawbacks of camping. We stayed in cabins with all the amenities and occupied ourselves with singing, fishing, tie-dyeing, reading, and swimming. However, the bedside manner of ER personnel impeded our Saturday night fireside chat with marshmallows. Robert required four sutures in his forehead after hitting his head on the swimming pool ladder.

Nonetheless, Robert was able to go into his July surgery with a load off his mind. In June, he signed a contingent contract to sell his office building and he applied for a rehabilitation engineering job in West Palm Beach. Finally, he had hope for putting his business woes behind him. Once again, Robert self-donated blood for the July hip-replacement surgery. However, this time he fainted after giving the first half-pint. Plan B involved cousins Susan and Tommy each donating a pint designated for Robert.

Dr. Matejcyk reported a good outcome after the three-hour surgery. However, the day after surgery Robert could barely stay awake. Tests showed a low blood count which was immediately remedied with another pint of blood. Despite being drowsy, Robert was alert enough to have the nurse check the donor's name on the blood bag. He relaxed when he learned he was getting Tommy's pint.

Despite this setback, Robert stayed on schedule with his therapy and made himself comfortable in a reclining pediatric wheelchair. He sat in the wheelchair for meals, could regularly adjust his position, and needed less help from nursing staff. Four days after surgery he was discharged.

Upon returning home, the house was ready for Robert and he resigned himself to two more weeks of house arrest. This time he used his computer while reclining on a daybed, entering data with voice-recognition software, and learned how to create a business website.

I had married Robert for richer or poorer, better or worse, but did not know it would be for shorter or taller. The prosthetic hip implants added one inch to his height. The moustache he had when we married also grew into a full beard—totally unplanned. When Robert forgot to bring his electric razor to the hospital, a hand razor was off limits for three weeks because he was on a blood thinner. We couldn't decide if the resulting beard gave him the look of a distinguished professor or a garden gnome. Comments from the family three months later, like "old man" and "All you are missing are the turned-up shoes," no doubt contributed to Robert's decision to shave the beard.

Closer or Farther

The week after Robert came home from the hospital, he received a job interview invitation from Florida. Such a trip was out of the question. However, because of an informal meeting he had prior to surgery, a telephone interview was substituted for an in-person formal interview. The job offer came in September. Robert did not hesitate to accept it.

The question remained, *What about me?*

When Robert said he was going to apply for the rehabilitation engineering job in West Palm Beach, I asked him, "What happens if you get the job?"

With no hesitation he said, "We'll move to Florida."

I snipped back, "And when do we get to talk about it?"

Robert did not see anything left to talk about because we had already agreed to put Rochester's long, cold, snowy winters behind us. We had discussed moving to where one of us had family—New Zealand, Australia, or Florida. My plan had been to explore the employment potential of all three locations and base our decision on the best option for both of us. Florida was my least favorite pick, especially since Robert knew I would hate the heat, mosquitoes, bugs and snakes. (New Zealand has no snakes.)

When Robert got the Florida job offer, his search ended—but for me it was only the beginning. I was not ready to move and start over again. I enjoyed my job, being an expert in disability law and making a decent salary. I had no interest in taking another state bar exam. Yet how could I ignore God's intervention in finding a buyer for the office building and in writing a job description with Robert's name all over it?

I was disappointed not to be moving closer to my family, but I reluctantly submitted to God's direction and Robert's desire. In return, Robert agreed to be the lead breadwinner and not to ask me to take the Florida bar exam. After qualifying to practice law in New Zealand, Ohio, and New York—I did not have another bar exam in me.

The worst part of leaving Rochester was leaving our church. On October 26, 1997, an after-church reception in our honor reminded us how much love and joy we had shared with so many at West Side Baptist church in the last nine years. Many people wished us God's blessings. One friend commented she found it hard to imagine West Side without us. We also found it hard to imagine life without West Side. We had a deep sense of gratitude as we pondered the positive influence this church community had in our spiritual development and the maturity of our marriage relationship.

The blessings continued as many church members helped us sort, toss, clean, and pack. We thanked God for the privilege of being part of this church. There were many cards of friendship, farewell, and parting prayers like the following:

I pray that you and Robert will always be in the center of His will.
May God's richest blessings and overflowing joy be yours forever.
Praying that you will feel our Lord's guidance and His arms around you. Above all, trust Him. He is faithful.

Robert was certainly experiencing blessings and joy. He could sleep through the night. He could walk and stand without pain in his hips. He only needed crutches for distance, uneven surfaces, speed, or at the end of a long day. In November 1997 he moved to Florida and reported for work at the Florida State Department of Labor, Division of Vocational Rehabilitation.

I stayed in Rochester until the end of February 1998 to wrap up my work, close on the office building, sell the house, and organize the move. The extra months gave me the emotional time I needed to say goodbye and do a Bible study on the book of Jonah—a critical study for me as I fought against where God was sending me. Thankfully, I got the message before being thrown overboard!

Chapter 16
Whose Plan Is It Anyway?

Arrivals

My 1998 arrival in Lake Worth was comparable to my friend Julie's arrival in West Palm Beach the same year. When we went to pick her up at the railway station, we discovered that the producers of *The Last Marshall* movie had changed the station's sign to read *Welcome to Miami*. Likewise, I arrived at the intended destination, but God had changed the sign to read *Welcome to My plans*. But this was no movie. It was a time to watch our plans fall apart and for us to change to God's plans. As I read in His word,

> *The LORD of hosts has sworn saying, "Surely, just as I have intended so it has happened, and just as I have planned so it will stand, . . .*
> *For the LORD of hosts has planned, and who can frustrate it? And as for His stretched-out hand, who can turn it back?"* ∞ *Isaiah 14:24, 27*

Living Arrangements

Buying a house was the first plan to fall. Robert decided to wait until his employment status moved from probationary to permanent before making this commitment. Although the rationale made sense, it was still disappointing to extend our wait another three months.

Living in privacy was the second plan to go down. As the executrix on the estate of her friend Jack, Paula persuaded Robert to move into Jack's house. I would have preferred to join Robert in the one-bedroom cottage where he had lived for three months while I transitioned from Rochester. I knew Jack's place would be like living in a museum with many collections and visitors. Stifling my concerns, I gave in, and moved in.

Even eating food from the cupboards proved inadvisable. Robert's young nephew John discovered this when I fed him cereal from Jack's kitchen as his after-school snack. John was playing with the cereal and studying it closely when I asked him what was wrong. He said there was something in it. I was skeptical until he showed me the live weevils swimming in the milk!

Jack's place was like a railway station with lots of arrivals and departures related to winding up his estate. Although Paula was very generous with her time and the rental arrangement, many interruptions made my work from a home office very difficult. Also, it was hard for both of us living with most of our personal items in storage.

Despite our living arrangements, we did benefit from being close to family. We enjoyed regular meals with Paula's family, watched the blossoming romance of one nephew, attended the high school graduation of another nephew, and began a Mother's Day tradition of enjoying brunch with a cousin's family at a local restaurant. Also, Robert enjoyed fishing with his brothers.

Job Frustrations

Robert's plan for a satisfying career as a rehabilitation engineer without the worries of private practice was also frustrated. It was a positive experience being part of Florida's Rehabilitation Engineering technology team, but there were local staffing issues. His assistant lacked the aptitude, attitude, and application to get the job done. She worked a maximum of two hours a day and either did not talk to Robert at all or failed to follow his directions. As a result, the cases began to backlog. Initially his boss characterized the problem as one of time and case management and a strong difference in work styles. Robert saw the difference as being one where he put out maximum effort and the assistant put out minimum effort. His boss refused to deal with the problem.

The job caused Robert extreme stress. He got many headaches and wanted to quit and have me get a job in a law firm. I reminded him of his promise to be the breadwinner and not to ask me to take the Florida bar exam. He reluctantly agreed to hang in there for a year. I was reminded of this Scripture:

> *Consider it pure joy, my brothers, whenever you face trials of many kinds, because you know that the testing of your faith develops perseverance. Perseverance must finish its work so that you may be mature and complete, not lacking anything. ∞ James 1:2-4, NIV*

My plan to maintain expertise in disability discrimination law by writing for Thomson Reuters as a contractor was also torpedoed. Three Americans with Disabilities writing contracts were not proffered: (1) the monthly newsletter; (2) a replacement chapter; and (3) the second edition of a single volume textbook. Although contract work was available, it was unrelated to disability law and of no interest to me. This time God spoke to me through the prophet Isaiah:

> *"Forget the former things; do not dwell on the past. See,*
> *I am doing a new thing! Now it springs up; do you not perceive it?*
> *I am making a way in the desert and streams in the wasteland. . . ."*
> *"I am the LORD your God, who teaches you what is best for you,*
> *who directs you in the way you should go. . . ."*
> ∞ *Isaiah 43:18, 19, 48:17b, NIV*

At the same time, I was learning lessons of humility and submission from studying 1 Peter in Bible Study Fellowship, an interdenominational Bible study. I struggled with God's timing in revealing His plan for us, but learned that impatience was clear evidence of a lack of submission.

Uncertainty

I was further humbled by the need for breast biopsies on two lumps, one in each breast. In the two-week delay between discovery of the lumps and the biopsy results, I wondered if *this was it* for me. Robert's idea of a joke was to ask if I still had life insurance—I was not amused. Thankfully, the lumps were cysts and not cancer.

In all the uncertainty of Robert's job and our temporary living quarters, we alternated between two churches. Robert was unwilling to join either one until we bought a house. This sounded reasonable when we thought we would be in our own home by May 1998, but when our temporary status continued all year, we failed to get involved in either church. This stifled both our Christian fellowship and involvement in ministry.

Visiting New Zealand and Australia Family and Friends

The move to Florida also changed our plans to visit my family in New Zealand and Australia. Robert had not accrued enough vacation time to make the trip and his work problems prevented me leaving him alone. However, I knew it was time to go home when Carolyn, a NZ friend, had an inoperable brain tumor with weeks to live. After much vacillation, Robert very reluctantly agreed for me to go without him.

It was not exactly a fun vacation. I not only visited Carolyn, but also my grandmother whose dementia had all but taken her away from the events and people around her.

At one point, Nana said, "God-only-knows where I am."

I answered, "You're right Nana, God does know where you are."

Her eyes lit up for a cognitive moment when she looked me straight in the eye and said, "You're right Angela, He probably does."

Another highlight was spending Fathers' Day with Dad for the first time in more than 20 years. This was possible because he came to Sydney with me to relax with the families of my brother, Greg, and sister, Deborah.

Thirty-six hours after leaving Sydney, Greg, Julie, Holly, and Sam joined us in Florida. The plan had been for us to be living in our own home by the time of their September visit. Instead, we were still at Jack's place contending with a sale of collectibles the morning after their arrival. We resolved the problem at a beachfront hotel with a pool for two nights. Otherwise, they bunked in with us at Jack's place in between trips to Florida tourist attractions. Their departure was especially tough after spending two solid months together.

Another Change in Direction

In the fall of 1998, in a remarkable turn of events, a decision was made to transfer Robert's problem assistant and for him to have input on her replacement. We also signed a contract to buy a house in Lake Clarke Shores and ordered a live Christmas tree in expectation of a December move-in date. God, again, had other plans.

Hurricane Mitch unleashed 24 hours of torrential rain just before the inspection, a perfect scenario for finding roof damage. Home inspections did reveal problems with the roof—and with the sprinklers, driveway, screens, window cranks, ceiling, and air conditioner. A more-detailed roof inspection uncovered multiple leaks and massive wood rot requiring a total roof replacement.

As Robert's brother Peter said, "Wow, God must be looking out for you guys."

The seller was unwilling to replace the roof so we terminated the contract and canceled the Christmas tree. That wasn't my only disappointment in the winter of 1998.

When the promise of a new assistant never materialized, Robert was ready to resign his job with the state and accept an offer to work as comptroller in a construction business in Stuart, Florida. I was not happy about this at all. I had sacrificed too much—so he could have this ideal job—only to watch him walk away one year later. It also made no sense to me that Robert would give up his rehabilitation engineering career to work in a construction business. I feared the consequences of the job not working out and the negative effect on his close relationship with his employer. I got Robert to pause long enough to consider the pros and cons, but there was no holding him back. Robert was so keen to get out of the state bureaucracy, he did not hesitate to accept this new offer. He resigned at the end of December 1998, and began the new year with the construction company.

Chapter 17
Putting Down Roots

Improvements

Although Robert's job change involved moving about 45 miles north from Lake Worth to Stuart, it did not affect my work-at-home situation. If anything, my work environment improved since we rented a small three-bedroom house that allowed me to use one of the bedrooms as a private office.

Our living situation also improved since our multi-tier platforms worked better in the compact kitchen giving us access to all but one lower cupboard. We also gained access to items we'd had in storage for a year, and the attached garage and utility room stored unpacked boxes. This house had a pool—a huge bonus—and an abundant supply of citrus fruit in the backyard. It thrilled us to send guests home with grapefruit and oranges.

Robert was pleased with his job change. He enjoyed setting up the business computers and was ready to train staff on the computer system by February. But one office worker was very vocal in resisting the change, and getting his employer to sit down and learn the computer program was harder than Robert anticipated. Even so, he remained confident the boss was on board with the new system and would direct staff to use it.

Building Our Own Home

In Stuart, our plan was to rent until we bought a lot on which to build a house to our own specifications. This was viable since property was more affordable in Martin County than Palm Beach County and we now lived close to family in the building trade. We could also work with Charlie, a custom homebuilder and high school family friend.

After three months of looking, we could not find a lot that met both our criteria. I wanted property with city water, a sewer connection, and a small yard; Robert wanted property with a water view and a southern exposure for warming a swimming pool. Lacking the finances to live on the ocean, the inner-coastal, or the river, Robert settled for a man-made lakefront property. Although we found a one-acre lot with no connections to city water or sewage (and a far cry from the limited landscaping I preferred), the lot was both serene and private. Robert loved it. I agreed on the condition that he would be the one to maintain the septic tank and well-water system.

I found the lot just before it went on the market. I talked to the owner in West Virginia and sensed that she was just as concerned to get a good neighbor for her daughter who lived next door as she was to get a good price. As a result, I sent her a personal letter with our written financial offer. We told the owner about ourselves: how long we had been married, why we moved to Florida, our involvement in church and disability advocacy, and our professional qualifications and employment. It was the right move. The owner was satisfied that we were suitable neighbors— she even knew some little people in her hometown—and the son-in-law negotiated a sale price that satisfied everyone.

Before we started building, many people warned us about the toll the process could have on our marriage. Although we did not become another divorce statistic, our commitment was tested a few times. We easily agreed on the ultimate goal of making the house accessible— wider door thresholds, no stairs, lower counters and windows, and roll-in showers. We spent hours at Barnes and Noble perusing building plan books. Robert incorporated our ideas into computer-generated draft building plans that we took to a licensed civil engineer to prepare for local permit approval. However, building could not begin until the county approved health and building permits, which took three months.

Finding God's Plan for My Job

After a 12-month, step-by-step separation from legal publishing, the last straw came when the publisher I contracted for reduced the compensation rate by 15%.

In February 1999, I declined a writing contract and said, "If I'm going to work for next to nothing, I'd rather donate my time to a worthy cause than to a greedy corporation."

Besides, it was not just about the money. I was bored with the material and working below my skill level.

Whatever the future, I knew that God brought us both to Florida and that He would provide for both of our careers. My Bible study in Genesis was helpful in giving one example after another of God providing for His people. It was a matter of trusting God to show me His plan and then being obedient to follow it. I began looking for other work. There were many possibilities:

- Contract with other legal publishers
- Obtain employment with a local legal publisher
- Clerk for a judge
- Write briefs and memorandum for private law firms
- Train as a mediator
- Pursue the executive director position with LPA
- Study for the Florida bar and work as an attorney in a law firm

Of course, the last item was the least attractive option. It was incredible to discover that God added another option to the list. I had been introduced to a worthy cause when the Christian Law Association (CLA) presented their mission at the church we attended in Lantana, Florida. When my disenchantment with secular legal publishing reached its peak in March, I offered my services as a contract writer to the CLA, a nationwide legal ministry dedicated to defending Christian liberty in America.

The timing was perfect. CLA was in need of a legal writer and invited me to their April 1999 seminar in Orlando. It was an opportunity for me to learn more about the free legal services available to Christian churches, pastors, schools, ministries, and individuals who experience religious discrimination.[1] The most I was hoping for was a contract offer. Instead, it was another realization from Ephesians:

Now to Him who is able to do far more abundantly beyond all that we
ask or think, according to the power that works within us, . . .
∞ *Ephesians 3:20*

At the end of the day, David Gibbs III said he believed God had sent me to the ministry and he made a conditional job offer—on the spot. The final offer was made after Robert and I visited the Seminole office for a more in-depth interview.

My tenure with CLA began on May 24, 1999. Technology made it possible for me to telecommute from my home office in Stuart to the CLA office in Seminole, Florida. Better yet, my talent was going to a worthy cause. Every morning at 8:30 a.m., I joined CLA staff by phone for a half-hour of devotions. Occasionally, I went to the Seminole office for staff meetings and to train summer interns. As a legal researcher and writer, I wrote and edited newsletter articles, seminar materials, pamphlets, books, draft radio scripts, and other publications under the names of David C. Gibbs Jr. or David C. Gibbs III.

Church Roots

Moving to Stuart put us back in the market for a church. Thankfully, it did not take long to feel comfortable at Tropical Farms Baptist Church. We liked the people, the pastor, the doctrine, and the emphasis on missions. We didn't want to make the mistake of alternating between churches as we did when living in Lake Worth and so, in the fall of 1999, we put down roots by joining this friendly fellowship.

Soon afterwards, Pastor Darrell Pace resigned to go into mission work in Bosnia. I served on the pastor search committee as a representative of new church members. In our nine months of weekly meetings, we never missed an opportunity to laugh. Jim was usually the ringleader, so one night—in his absence—we slipped in an extra sheet of candidate interview questions. The following week we asked for Jim's approval of the questions. He quizzically read a series of personal and irrelevant questions, such as:

- *Do you shower in the morning or evening?*
- *What brand of toothpaste do you use?*
- *Have you ever whipped a dead horse?*

When Jim read the dead horse question, he got the joke; *hating to whip a dead horse* was his trademark introduction to reiterating a point.

Robert served on a monthly rotation as a church money counter. He enjoyed the challenge and initiated a review of the procedures with the guidance of a CLA publication on the subject.

Robert's Job Insecurity and House Construction

As the year progressed, Robert's optimism for computerizing his employer's construction business faded. His employer never sat down to learn the system and he let staff bypass the computer and continue doing things by hand. Inevitably, this created enormous tension and inefficiencies for the business. By the time our house construction began in September, a huge question mark hung over Robert's future in the business. We prayed that we could at least get the house finished before things fell apart completely.

In contrast, Charlie, our building contractor, was a delight to work with. If subcontractors made mistakes, Charlie took care of it. For example, when the block layers did not follow the plans, Charlie had them remove the two extra rows of blocks that set the window openings too high. He was very flexible as we selected windows, doors, roof shingles, tiles, paint colors, countertops, carpet, fixtures, appliances, and subcontractors to build the kitchen cabinets and the pool.

Charlie was amazing when he achieved the almost impossible and obtained the certificate of occupancy on December 30th so that we could move in on December 31, 1999. In order to claim the homestead tax exemption in the year 2000 we needed to be living in the house on January 1st. We cut it so close that when the moving truck arrived at the house, workers were still laying carpet, installing closet shelving, and cleaning floors. After filling the garage, the truck contents were temporarily unloaded onto the driveway.

A few months earlier, we had hosted a Y2K party with cousins Lyn and Bill where we encouraged family members to prepare for the worst, hope for the best, and trust God for the rest. We recommended preparations for possible power, food, and water shortages.

We began the 21st century in our new home and woke up with great anticipation on January 1, 2000. Would there be electricity? Would there be running water? Would the millennium bug bring the chaos predicted? The answers lay in the simple flick of the light switch.

And There was Light!

We were so grateful to wake up to the best-case scenario on January 1, 2000. Even so, our preparations were not wasted—it was good training for future weather-related emergencies. The Y2K planning exercise also gave us an appreciation for the daily comforts that we take for granted. In the short term, we greatly reduced our grocery bill as we used up our emergency supply of canned and dry food.

Our arrival came to the immediate attention of the homeowners' association (HOA). They had no objection to the team of 20 church and family volunteers that helped us move, but rather to a covenant violation of moving in before we laid the sod. Unfortunately, we almost lost the entire lawn when the pump and sprinkler system malfunctioned. In addition, the well was sucking too much sand and we had to hook up to our neighbor's well for 10 days while our well was surged. Thankfully, this did not spoil our classification as good neighbors for the former owner's daughter and the HOA was satisfied when our sod was laid a few days later.

We had finally put down roots in a Florida church and home, and I was settled in my job. The question was whether Robert's roots in the construction business would stay planted.

Chapter 18
Returning to Familiar Territory

Unemployed Again

Robert did everything he could to put down roots in the construction business, yet in February 2000, he was among several laid-off employees. The loss of a major business contract allowed everyone to save face in explaining Robert's departure from the business. Nonetheless, Robert was disappointed that his employer diminished the value of his computer skills and contribution to the business.

At the same time, we were relieved and grateful for God's timing in allowing Robert to keep his job until our house construction was complete. In addition, my employer CLA generously added Robert to the employee health plan without any payroll deduction. It also helped that Robert was eligible to collect unemployment compensation.

Computer Skills Confirmed

After six months, Robert accepted a part-time job teaching computer skills at a Christian residential school for boys. Robert taught the boys for a year. He also repaired numerous donated computers for the children. The job was not what Robert had in mind and the pay could not sustain him in the long term, but clearly God picked Robert for this temporary assignment—He showed Robert that his computer skills did have value. God confirmed this to me at my Monday night class for Bible Study Fellowship. One of the women in my discussion group was the wife of the director of the same residential school.

Reactivation of Adaptive Living

When no local rehabilitation engineering jobs came through, Robert reactivated his rehabilitation engineering practice. Adaptive Living acquired its own domain name, increased marketing of the Ergo Chair for little people—which he had continued as a side business in Florida— and eventually delivered rehabilitation engineering consulting services again. Much of Robert's consulting work was with the State of Florida's Medicaid Waiver programs for Home and Community-Based Services for Developmental Disabilities and Brain and Spinal Cord Injury. Robert focused on home modifications. This enabled families to continue caring for loved ones at home to avoid institutionalization or homelessness.

Participating in the expo at the annual LPA national conferences was the best way for Adaptive Living to market the Ergo Chair.[1] This gave little people the opportunity to adjust the chair to their unique shape and be photographed sitting in the chair. Many took that image back to their employer or school district to show why Ergo Chair was the accommodation they needed.

On October 31, 2000, Robert demonstrated an old talent by enhancing his photography with an original poem:

It's our anniversary.
Rejoice in the warmth of our love and life together
as the wild flowers of Mount Hood show their brilliance
and delicate beauty over the landscape.
So shall we as a couple shine the light of our faith and kindness
to the world.

Dear Angela
As the years go by, I will always love you and appreciate you in my life as my wife! Our marriage will always be based on a loving understanding and strong Christian ideals.
Happy Anniversary
Love, Robert

The year 2001 began well as we enjoyed the month of January in New Zealand. A rental car gave us the independence needed to connect with friends throughout the North Island. Robert was thrilled with his catch of three trout in Lake Taupo and seeing a long-distance view of a *Lord of the Rings* film set before it was dismantled. [2]

Whangamata was a familiar haven for two weeks. We returned to the place of my childhood summer vacations with family. We relived many experiences at the beach, the Harbor Lookout on Te Karaka Point, Wentworth Valley, Opoutere, the small community church, and the same old movie house in town. We enjoyed fish and chips served in a newspaper wrapping, smoked fish, and Tuatua[3] fritters. Robert took us on a wild goose chase looking for gold in the Karangahake Gorge. We even had a traditional family concert.

Inevitably, a few things had changed. Everyone was checking email and we were now the generation stocking the fridge, preparing meals, and monitoring the activities of the teenagers. As part owners of the beach house, there were also a few items of business needing our attention.

Muir families at Whangamata beach house

We returned to the United States refreshed and ready to work. I continued to research, write, and edit for CLA.[4] In addition to publishing activities, other work responsibilities kept me busy and fulfilled, namely:

- Presenting the CLA ministry to churches
- Training summer interns
- Acquiring Continuing Legal Education credits at Christian Legal Society conferences in Destin, Florida and Savannah, Georgia
- Joining staff at spiritual emphasis conferences

Past Issues Resurfaced

Two issues from the past resurfaced in 2002. First, the doctor that had ended Robert's career in dwarfism medical research passed away after an extensive cancer battle. His death brought an outpouring of love, gratitude, and devotion from patients, family, and friends. So many described how his extraordinary skill as a surgeon had given them mobility without pain and hope for a brighter future. Just as significant were his friendship, compassion, care, and encouragement. Many memorialized him as gentle, kind, patient, humble, a legend, a saint, and a hero.

Although we had witnessed many of these traits in the doctor, we had also seen his limitations. Almost 20 years later, it was still painful to remember how the doctor broke trust with Robert in mailing a fundraising letter and how abruptly their professional and personal relationship ended. Robert still mourned the loss of what could have been—the unrealized vision of the doctor going beyond filling waiting rooms with patients to stacking library shelves with medical books he wrote for the generations to come. Instead, the doctor took his vast experience and understanding of dwarfism with him to the grave. I mentioned that when the doctor sent us flowers after Robert's resignation, it had felt like a virtual funeral—now it was the real thing. We had no more time to restore the broken relationship. Although I had forgiven the doctor in my heart, I still regret not writing to tell him so.

Marriage conflict was the second issue to return. The dispute centered on ownership of a boat that came to Robert via a family connection. This was the same boat we had borrowed from his brother Mickey five years earlier for the trip to John Pennekamp in Key Largo.

At the time, Mickey had reminded Robert and his nephew, David, "Don't forget to put the drain plugs in."

They learned the importance of that warning as they watched the boat sinking at the boat ramp.

I was opposed to Robert owning the boat because of the cost of insurance, storage, and maintenance. I finally relented when Robert agreed to a budget cap. However, as anticipated, Robert far exceeded the cap. I fussed and argued with him about it many times, but those were wasted words.

Finally, God gave me a solution. Stop complaining about boat expenses and get Robert to agree that for every dollar he spends on the boat, I could spend a dollar on whatever I wanted without discussing it with him. It worked. The arguments stopped and I enjoyed the freedom of having a sizable discretionary fund at my disposal.

I named the boat *Cork It* after another boat sinking fiasco. Once corking the boat became routine, Robert had fun fishing and playing tour guide in the inner coastal waterways to various family members. Even I enjoyed the day we docked at one restaurant for soup and another for the entrée. Despite being wind-blown and covered in sea salt, we were refreshed and invigorated.

Eventually Robert came to his senses and saw that boat ownership was more than he bargained for. Not only did it cost him more than he wanted to pay, but also, he could not physically manage the boat without help. In time, Robert transferred the title to his niece Veronica. I was glad to see Robert put a final cork in his boat expenses and return to discussing and agreeing on financial matters.

Chapter 19

Everything Broke Loose

September 11, 2001

One morning I was in a quandary during CLA devotions. It was my turn to share and I could not pick one thing for which I was thankful. My hesitancy was not due to ingratitude, rather being overwhelmed with so much to appreciate. I had a loving husband and family, a great church, a lovely home, interesting work, and good health. I was obviously thankful in good times, but soon I would learn how to be thankful in tough times.

September 11 stopped us all in our tracks as we saw the twin towers of the World Trade Center tumble, the Pentagon in flames, and the debris of United Flight 93 in a Pennsylvania field. The shock, the grief, and the pain were overwhelming. Robert's distress caused his September 12 admission to the Jupiter Medical Center for two nights with a suspected heart attack. Thankfully, tests didn't show any heart problems—apparently, he had an anxiety attack. And an overdose of the diagnostic medication gave him a massive migraine that kept him an extra night in the hospital.

Like most Christians, I was thrilled at the thousands who turned to God for hope and comfort in the aftermath of 9/11. The churches were full. Public prayers were common. But when church soon dropped off the weekly schedule of these newcomers, I was sad that America's focus on God was so short-lived. Did they not know that prayer is not reserved for crisis? God longs for a relationship with us in both the good times and the bad. When troubles come our way, we pray for God to remember us, but when things are going well how quickly we forget God's goodness.

Skirting Hurricanes on Caribbean Cruise

In the fall of 2002, we dodged disaster in the waters of the Western Caribbean. As a crew member, my niece Nadia got free fare for her parents, sister, and grandfather, and half-fare for Robert and me. Nadia and her dance partner, Chris, entertained more than 2,000 passengers in the featured adage (slow and controlled ballet movements performed with grace and fluidity). Naturally, this was the highlight of our week, especially since they performed in two different shows every night.

Nadia hosts family in guest dining room

Robert added an experiment to the mix. He shaved off his beard over a period of three days: first the moustache, then the goatee, and finally the sideburns. No one noticed until it was all gone. My excuse is that he was out gallivanting on the ship so much, I hardly saw him. He even joined some honeymoon couples for the midnight buffet.

Hurricanes Isidore and Lili had tried to rob us of this family vacation. Isidore crossed the Yucatan Peninsula as a Category 2 hurricane, but weakened to a tropical storm when it hit New Orleans, our port of departure. We sailed on time. Then Lili hit our ports of call in Jamaica and the Cayman Islands as a Category 1 hurricane. As the ship listed to one side, Robert propelled his wheelchair with one hand. Lili caused Georgetown Port to close to all cruise ships, and caused the stingrays to miss Robert swimming with them at Grand Cayman. Instead, he visited tropical fish at Doctor's Cave Beach Club reef in Montego Bay, Jamaica.

Our ship headed south to avoid hurricane weather as Lili stormed up the Gulf of Mexico. When Lili reached Category 4 status, 850,000 people in Louisiana received evacuation orders. Dan Rather, the CBS anchor at the time, stood on the dock in New Orleans and asked if this was *the big one*.[1] There was a collective sigh of relief when she weakened to a Category 2 hurricane.

Dark Cloud Hung Over Our Church

On March 19, 2003, it felt like the big one had hit our church family in Stuart, Florida. On the same day the United States went to war with Iraq, Pastor Dave of Tropical Farms Baptist Church resigned. The gasp of agony his wife, Lea, let out when she heard Dave's words of resignation ripped right through me. I was heartbroken, as I had served on the pastor search committee and knew God had spoken clearly in calling Dave to our church in September 2000.

The storm watch had occurred a month earlier when four of six church deacons resigned. Pastor Dave stood on the Bible with his belief that as the church shepherd he had authority to make unilateral decisions. In contrast, deacons and church members believed in pastoral leadership balanced by membership consensus.

In the month prior to Pastor Dave's resignation, Robert and I tried to de-escalate the conflict by meeting with Pastor Dave, deacons, and some pastor search committee members. But by the time of the March 19 special church business meeting, the storm status had moved from a watch to a warning. The tension bubbling beneath the surface boiled over in the meeting as people expressed concern, confusion, and criticism. Although there was a plea for compromise, better communication, and reconciliation, no one was ready to vote for the motion I brought—to contract with a church mediator. Instead, Pastor Dave resigned and walked out of the business meeting. In the wake of the storm, several members followed him and split the church.

Pastor Paul's sermon on March 24, 2003, stopped Robert and me from also leaving the church. He preached from the Psalms on "How to Handle Life's Hurts."

The Holy Spirit convicted me when Pastor Paul said, "We cannot run away from pain. When God calls us to something, we do not have the choice to run. The problem will follow wherever we go. The remedy is to give it to God."

Thus, we followed the psalmist's example and cried out to God:
I cry aloud with my voice to the LORD; I make supplication with my voice to the LORD. I pour out my complaint before Him; I declare my trouble before Him. ∞ *Psalm 142:2-3*

At the same time, I was dealing with suspicious lumps found in a routine mammogram and ultrasound. God was gracious when a needle aspiration caused the dark spots to disappear off the screen. Unfortunately, no such aspiration alleviated the dark cloud hanging over our church.

As the designated church liaison, I sought the conflict resolution and Leader Care resources of the Florida Baptist Convention office in Jacksonville. Sadly, Pastor Dave declined to participate in mediation. The church then engaged Director Bob of Leader Care to help us enter a severance agreement with Pastor Dave and to seek healing and reconciliation before calling another pastor. The church met with Director Bob on March 27, 2003, the same day as Uncle Chuck's Memorial service; he had died a month earlier in Alabama at the age of 89.

Death of Beloved Aunts and Uncles

Uncle Chuck was one of Robert's greatest cheerleaders. He opened Robert's eyes to God's country—the USA that Uncle Chuck saw during the depression and the conservative political views he carried to the end of his days. He taught Robert to enjoy the simple pleasures of playing card games like Pinochle and 500, and taking in God's creation. They drove thousands of miles together on several cross-country trips. Along the way, they enjoyed five National Parks and stopped at many hospitals—not due to any emergency, rather because hospital cafeterias were Uncle Chuck's budget pick for a cheap and nutritious meal.

We needed further comfort on April 2, 2003, when we got news that my Auntie Nan had terminal lung cancer with only a few weeks to live. At age 85, Nan declined treatment and chose palliative care in a nursing home with a private room, a lovely view of the gardens, and access to her traditional pre-dinner sherry.

Only two weeks earlier, we had booked nonrefundable tickets for a July NZ trip. However, it would be too late to visit Nan if we waited until July. We agreed I should go on to New Zealand in May, but not on a vacation. I worked by extending my remote link with the CLA office from about 200 miles to more than 8,000. We'd made the right decision. Within three days of my return to Florida, Nan passed away. Although I could not be at the funeral, I helped my sister, Deborah, write the eulogy she delivered on behalf of our family. Nan's 1959 profession of faith in

Jesus Christ at the NZ Billy Graham Crusade had influenced our family down to the third generation. That assurance was the reason Nan was at peace and ready to meet her Lord.

In December 2005, Robert was able to use his storytelling gift when giving the eulogy for Uncle Bob, his godfather, namesake, and mentor. Family and priests alike did not know what to expect when Robert stood on the podium in a Catholic church with a toolbox from which he pulled two metal pipes and a soldering torch. He used the tools of Uncle Bob's trade to demonstrate key aspects of his faith, character, life, and marriage. A fitting tribute, indeed.

Health Problems

In July and August 2003, Robert and I both made our planned trip to New Zealand and Australia. The 50° drop in temperature shocked Robert. Likewise, Dad was shocked when Robert used a two-month supply of kerosene for the heater in only three days.

As a rude reminder of my advancing years, I fell and severely sprained my wrist the day before we flew home from Sydney. I had one night to ice it, then fellow passengers across the Pacific suffered with me as I massaged my wrist with the penetrating and aromatic goanna extra-strength heat cream. The healing process was impeded by the need to continue lifting myself on and off chairs, toilets, and in and out of the car.

Actually, the wrist was only part of my physical troubles. For some time, I had been losing range of motion in my ankles. This painful issue interrupted my sleep, reduced my already limited walking distance, made stairs and curbs impossible to climb without a railing, and required avoidance of uneven surfaces like grass and gravel. At the end of August, I finally went to a local orthopedist to get x-rays. He pronounced severe arthritis and was amazed that I could walk at all. He was happy to write a prescription for a scooter and a lift to get it in and out of the car.

In September, I brought the x-rays to Dr. Mary Matejcyk, the same doctor who had done Robert's hip replacements in Cleveland, Ohio, in 1997. In another of God's divine appointments, she attended an LPA meeting in Gainesville, Florida. Dr. Matejcyk noted that the spontaneous fusion of my ankle joints was causing the pain. This sounds bad, but it was actually good news. Surgical intervention would be to fuse the joints, whereas my ankles were doing this on their own. The only concern was that the ankles fuse in the right position for standing and this appeared to be happening. The good news was that when the fusion was complete the pain would end. Instead of surgery, I now needed a scooter to increase my mobility.

Several family members also experienced physical problems in 2003:

- Robert's brother, Michael, had a stroke at age 52 years and ultimately had to leave work and go on disability.
- My father, Neil Muir, was hospitalized with a life-threatening bladder infection and stones requiring surgery a month later.
- Robert's Aunt Rita fell and broke her leg resulting in surgery and rehabilitation.

Robert had no health incidents in 2003. However, he got quite a scare on the scales at the doctor's office. The calibration on our home scale was off by seven pounds. We were both forced to admit we needed to lose weight to reduce stress on our joints.

CLA Staff Layoff

On September 10, 2003, a major funding source severed its ties with CLA. The staff waited in trepidation for how this would affect the ministry. Robert and I were on the verge of buying a car to replace my 11-year-old Honda when God warned me that there would be layoffs and I would be one of them. We heeded the warning and put off the car purchase.

On October 3, 2003, I got the call that I was in the 25% CLA staff layoff. The news was not upsetting because God had prepared us in advance. Despite the uncertainty that comes with unemployment, on the same day President Lincoln found things for which to be thankful 140 years earlier in the midst of a civil war,[2] I was thankful. I had the opportunity to work for a Christian law firm on religious liberty issues for four-and-a-half years. I was thankful for the relationships with my co-workers. I was thankful I would no longer work on a CLA book manuscript that sat unpublished. I was thankful Robert would stop complaining about my not getting credit for my writings. And, I was thankful I was now free to build my own professional reputation.

God's Provision

Robert also had losses to endure. In October, his computer crashed twice and he lost all data—even the backups. In November, outgoing mail was stolen from our mailbox, including checks paying numerous bills. The bank fees would have been too high to cancel the checks so Robert had to close the account and rewrite the stolen checks and other checks not yet presented for payment. I prayed for God's mercy:

Be gracious to me, O God, be gracious to me, For my soul takes refuge in You; And in the shadow of Your wings I will take refuge until destruction passes by. I will cry to God Most High, To God who accomplishes all things for me. He will send from heaven and save me; He reproaches him who tramples upon me. Selah. God will send forth His lovingkindness and His truth. ∞ Psalm 57:1-3

Weeks before we knew that I would be unemployed, God provided an extra source of income. Robert contracted with the American Association for the Advancement in Science (AAAS) to recruit Florida students with disabilities for the Entry Point! paid-internship summer program. It was a bonus for Robert to visit the University of Florida and the University of Central Florida, colleges from which he had graduated in the 1970s. A bonus for AAAS was Robert's role in recruiting two new internship employers, namely Merck and Google. Because this was only a part-time, short-term project, Robert continued selling Ergo Chairs for little people and providing rehabilitation engineering services to individuals with disabilities.

Chapter 20
Searches

Church Pastor

Almost six months after the resignation of Pastor Dave and in the 40th anniversary year of Tropical Farms Baptist (TFBC), the church was ready to begin the search for a new pastor. I accepted the invitation to serve as a member of the search committee. My responsibilities were to be diligent in prayer, consider the needs of the whole church, maintain confidentiality, persevere until God's choice was found, attend and prepare for regular meetings, meet and interview candidates, and check their references.

When I joined the pastor search committee in August 2003, I did not know that my own job search would begin in October. I was aware that I would bring experience from being on Pastor Dave's search committee, but God knew that I would also bring sensitivity to the candidate's situation. At the same time that I was reviewing resumes of pastors, I was writing and sending out my own resumes.

All six committee members were quickly drawn to the resume of one candidate in our stack of 18—with no debate. The Holy Spirit had planted one name in all our minds. We wanted to know more about him and eagerly listened to his sermon tapes. Only four months into our search, and the committee was already preparing interview questions.

In contrast, four months into my job search, I had sent 42 inquiries. There were a few nibbles of interest in my credentials, but none from organizations with funds to hire me. God's Word kept me going:

> *If the LORD had not been my help, My soul would soon have dwelt in the abode of silence. If I should say, "My foot has slipped," Your lovingkindness, O LORD, will hold me up. When my anxious thoughts multiply within me, Your consolations delight my soul. ∞ Psalm 94:17-19*

In January 2004, the pastoral search committee made a discreet visit to the candidate's home church. As a courtesy, we called him the night before to say we were coming. Protocol in these situations is for the visiting committee not to draw attention upon arrival at the church. Instead of walking in together or all sitting in the same row, we walked into the sanctuary in ones and twos and spread out among the congregation. However, Corrie and I did not escape attention. One church member quizzed us about where we were from and insisted on introducing us to the pastor. He greeted us graciously while no doubt guessing that we were among his under-the-radar guests.

The pastor search committee enjoyed the church service and was impressed with both the candidate's preaching and his gentleness. When the substitute song leader lost his place, the pastor quietly walked over and put his arm around his shoulder—the right touch at the right time. We did not hesitate to schedule interviews with the candidate, his wife, and multiple references. With the candidate's permission, we also conducted a criminal/credit background check.

After spending an informative and comfortable day together in February, we followed with a March 4th letter to church members announcing the committee's unanimous recommendation that Leland A. Fielder be the next pastor of TFBC. We praised God that Lee and his wife, Angie, also believed God was calling them to serve at our church.

Now it was up to the church membership to agree. The introduction of Lee and Angie to the members occurred on the weekend of March 20-21, 2004, with meetings, fellowships, a town-hall-type question-and-answer session, and preaching in the morning and evening services. Approval of the search committee's recommendation followed at the business meeting on March 24. Within a month, Pastor Lee and Angie began their ministry at Tropical Farms Baptist Church.

Angela's Job Search

In contrast, after six months, my job search continued and my unemployment compensation was about to end. I had sent out another 20 resumes and researched 64 potential employers. My hope for finding a work-at-home position writing for a Christian or humanitarian organization had all but dissipated. I was now open to all options. I applied for jobs outside the home, identified a course for training as a mediator, and still hoped to find work without taking the Florida Bar Exam. May 1st was the registration deadline for the July exam, so I made this a personal deadline. If nothing came through by then, I would reluctantly bite the bar-exam bullet again.

In March, I was a contender for two jobs in the nonprofit sector. Both jobs had appeal, as they were organizations serving people with disabilities. One had been in the hopper since January and the other had just advertised a vacancy. One application process was extremely involved requiring the completion of a detailed interview questionnaire and the other only asked for a resume that I submitted with one sentence on the fax cover sheet.

In preparing for the Stuart job interview three miles from our house, I went beyond due diligence and read board minutes, the grant proposal that funded the position, and broadcasted an email to Christian friends asking for prayer. For the West Palm Beach job with a 90-mile-round-trip commute, I invested one hour of preparation and only asked a few people to pray. Clearly, I hoped to get the job in Stuart.

However, when I was getting out of the car for the West Palm Beach job interview, I whimsically said to God, "Wouldn't it be funny if this is the job You want me to have?"

I found out that God does have a sense of humor.

I did not get the job in which I had invested so much time. Rather, I got the job that God prepared for me with minimal effort on my part. But that is not all. My interview in West Palm Beach was at the main office. I did not know that only two months earlier the agency had opened a satellite office in Stuart that was also about three miles from our house. My assignment was to the Stuart office. Then, I absolutely knew for sure that:

> *The mind of man plans his way, But the LORD directs his steps.*
> ∞ *Proverbs 16:9*

God definitely had the big picture in mind even when I had no idea what was going on. Many friends who prayed with me during the job search had shared my disappointments and even counseled that God must be guiding me towards something better. Now we praised God together for His magnificence. I accepted a position as an advocacy specialist for the Coalition for Independent Living Options, Inc. (CILO) in April and began work on May 17, 2004.

Chapter 21
Ministry and Hospitality

Residential Guests

Our Christian faith and church community at Tropical Farms Baptist Church was our anchor. The Bible teaching and Christian fellowship helped us deal with advocacy challenges—and everything else, for that matter. We continued in both hospitality and ministry. In 2002, our residential hospitality extended to 10- and 12-year-old brothers whose state-appointed guardian had surgery and there was nobody to care for them while he was in the hospital. Also that year, Robert's brother John and his 13-year-old daughter, Brittany, stayed with us for five weeks while John saved for an apartment security deposit.

The winter visit of Robert's cousin, Bob, from Indiana soon became an annual event. In 2004, Bob returned and was surprised to see that the pine tree his father hit when backing out of the driveway the year before was still alive. Bob and Robert talk and shop for computers and ham-radio parts. Bob is the model guest as he buys his own food, brings his own laundry detergent, and does his own laundry.

No, Robert's siblings are not little people

Hosting Events

Van Etten Woods has been the venue for many seasonal events, meetings and parties.

Robert's sister, Paula, described our place as the party house—the perfect place for a crowd.

Like many Florida homes, the great room with the nine-foot cathedral ceiling flows without walls from the kitchen into the dining room, sitting room, and living room. A large group can spill out onto the patio and pool area. There is room for lawn games and catch-and-release fishing in the lake. We counted more than 70 people at one family gathering, while a more comfortable crowd is closer to 30.

Although we have the room, we continue the style of hospitality we developed at the beginning of our marriage in Baltimore—with everyone sharing the work. Most events are potluck, and we have the perfect buffet setting for the food. Instead of hanging half our kitchen cabinets out of reach on the wall, all cabinets are set on the floor. They sit back-to-back with one set facing the kitchen and the other facing the living and dining rooms. The cabinet top facing away from the kitchen makes an ideal surface for a buffet spread.

The only stressor in preparing for an event is getting the house cleaned up for company. For me, the bonus is that Robert is motivated to clear his stuff off the counters and out of the guest bathroom. Clean-up after an event is easy as most everyone pitches in: helping with dishes, wiping down counters, taking out the garbage, or sometimes even cleaning floors. However, average-sized people are at a disadvantage leaning over to use the 23.5-inch height sink or stove top. Some sit on a chair or kneel and a few accept a kneeling cushion for comfort.

Covered dish meals are a tradition in church communities, which makes it easy for us to host church fellowships. We even hosted a surprise 70th birthday party for Frances, a remarkable Christian friend from our church. In her honor, I wrote a custom crossword with clues specific to her life. Frances had no family that would put a party together for her and I had no mother with whom to celebrate a 70th. Although momentarily speechless, by the time she wrote her thank-you card, Frances found the words to describe the party as *wonderful, super, and awesome.*

LPA gatherings traditionally include guests bringing a side dish. We enjoy hosting at least one South Florida Mini-Gators chapter meeting a year. It is great to see little people appreciating the accessible features of our home, especially the kitchen. Unfortunately, Hurricane Jeanne caused the cancellation of our September 2004 meeting.

As a result, we no longer host chapter meetings during hurricane season.

The neighbors became accustomed to our annual little people event. However, even we were surprised to see our friend Edna from Ohio ride in on her three-wheel adapted Harley Davidson motorbike. She was able to get leather garb to fit her LP body, but we were concerned that she could not get a motorbike helmet to fit her head.

International Guests

Wendy, a little person from New Zealand, was our guest for the first two weeks of May in 2004. We showed her the local sights and enjoyed Sea World and Universal Studios in Orlando, along with Robert's cousin, Brett. Naturally Wendy and I also reminisced on our younger years together as founding members of LPNZ in 1969. Wendy was taking this trip knowing that her mobility was in serious decline due to spinal stenosis. It would not be long before she would need a wheelchair for both short and long distances.

The visit of Etsuko Enami, a professional photographer from Japan, was another casualty of Hurricane Jeanne. Etsuko had to postpone her four-day September visit to December 2004. At first, I was feeling very inhospitable when I learned that her departure on Christmas Day would take a good chunk of this special day—driving over 200 miles to and from Miami International Airport. However, after discovering what a gracious and delightful guest she was, I was ashamed of such thoughts. Etsuko cooked us traditional Japanese food and gave us a copy of many photos she had taken of us in our daily routines.

Etsuko first learned about little people from American missionary John Lusk who ministered to Japanese little people.In 2005, her remarkable photo essay was published in the book called *Little People*.[1] Eight of the 184 pages featured Robert and me.[2] The most amusing photo was the one where Robert hiked his swimming trunks up to show off a hip-replacement scar. I was not home to advise against having this photo taken. The caption reads: *Many dwarfs have this bone problem and Robert is no exception.* We now refer to ourselves as having the bone problem.

Church Ministry

I continued my church ministry as the Sunday school director, a leader in the AWANA[3] children's program, the alternate moderator at church business meetings, and the Angel Tree Christmas gift coordinator for children of prisoners.[4] Personal Bible study was critical in helping me maintain my commitment to Christian discipleship and witness.

A couple of months after I was elected for a two-year term to the LPA executive committee in July 2004, Robert was elected for a three-year term as one of seven church deacons. In this role, he assisted the pastor, advised on daily church operations, and encouraged church families assigned to him. He continued teaching the senior men's Sunday school class named the Older Wiser Learners of Scripture (OWLS); he had been teaching the class since 2002.

As a deacon, Robert also had opportunities to pray and share in the Sunday morning worship service. He especially enjoyed bringing his stories to life. For example, one morning Robert told the Paul Harvey story, "Jesus and the Cage."[5] Like the pastor in the story, Robert brought an empty birdcage onto the podium. All eyes fixed on Robert as he told the story of the young boy who had used a birdcage to collect wild birds to tease, pull out their feathers, and feed to his cat when he got tired of them. A pastor paid the boy $10 for the birds and then set them free. Robert drew the parallel of Satan trapping and terrorizing people and Jesus paying the price to set us free. The story ended when Robert picked up the cage, opened the cage door, and walked from the podium.

We had always wanted to deepen our spiritual understanding by visiting the historic biblical sites in the Middle East. However, after various friends told us how inaccessible it was to wheelchairs and scooters, we crossed it off our list of things to do.

We settled for a visit to The Holy Land Experience, a living biblical museum, in Orlando, Florida. To our surprise, some of the exhibits were more interactive than we expected—like the camel that delighted in nibbling on Robert's ear. As you can imagine, Robert did not relish the experience as much as the camel. But he reluctantly held his position long enough for me to snap a photo.

*Hearing aids enhance sound of
camel slurping in Robert's ear*

*Mr. Adventure parasails over
the Straits of Florida*

Chapter 22
A Dose of Humility

More Hurricanes

Our initial attention to hurricane Katrina was purely self-interest. We were relieved on August 25th that she had not messed with our Key West plans, instead passing through North Miami Beach as a Category 1 hurricane. Once we emerged from flying high in Greg's 50th birthday bubble, we were sobered by the havoc wreaked on the Gulf Coast and the breaking of the New Orleans levees. Katrina, the largest residential disaster in US history, killed at least 986 Louisiana residents, displaced more than one million Gulf Coast residents, and caused about $135 billion

Family celebrates Greg's 50th

in damages.[1] We were gratified to belong to two organizations that responded in a practical way to the disaster: (1) the Southern Baptist Convention Disaster Relief of the North American Mission Board and (2) LPA.[2]

As our family prepared to leave Key West, we were jolted with the news that Janet's husband, Ray, had been rushed to the hospital in Nashville with a suspected heart attack. We delayed our departure to help Janet pack and take her to the airport for the next flight out. It was an answer to prayer when Ray made a full recovery.

On October 24, 2005, Key West did not fare so well when Hurricane Wilma hit with 120 mph winds. Thirty-five percent of the city streets were flooded with three to five feet of water.[3] Wilma made another landfall near Naples, Florida, as a Category 3 hurricane, crossed the state in under four hours, and hit Stuart[4] as a Category 2 hurricane with winds of 105 mph. We were among the six million Floridians from Key West to Daytona Beach that lost power.[5] The 2004 hurricanes had prepared us well for implementing our disaster plan. We were grateful to suffer only five days without power and running water.

One woman put it well when she said, "You just pretend like you're camping and you don't complain. We have a very spoiled society. This is a dose of humility." [6]

Although Wilma ranked as the third costliest hurricane in US history—estimates of insured losses ranged from $8 to $12 billion[7] —our damages were minimal. We merely lost a couple of fence segments, porch screens, and the top of one pine tree. God's protection was amazing given that Wilma destroyed over 1,000 homes in our county and caused $50 million of damages to residential properties.[8]

Within a week of surviving Hurricane Wilma, Robert almost went to be with his Maker. I was inside on the computer working on backlogged LPA work, and Robert was outside doing pool maintenance. I heard him coughing and spluttering and tried to ignore the distraction. But when the coughing was severe and constant, I had to investigate. Just as well I did—Robert had inhaled chlorine gas. Hurricane Wilma had wet the chlorine tablets and generated green poisonous gas in the bottom of the chlorine storage canister. Instead of holding his breath when he reached in to pull out the chlorine tablets, Robert inhaled while pondering the identity of the green stuff.

Continual coughing, spluttering, and advice from the poison control center finally convinced him to go to the hospital ER. We could both think of better things to do with four hours on the eve of our 24th wedding anniversary. Thankfully, a chest x-ray, three breathing treatments, and three days of prednisone pills took care of the problem. We celebrated God's favor and mercy. The Hallmark anniversary card I gave Robert the next day was more meaningful than ever:

It's been years since we started our voyage together . . . And the storms we've weathered have drawn us closer . . . I'm so glad that I decided to take the journey of a lifetime with you.

Still Learning How to Communicate

After 25 years, we both publicly embarrassed ourselves when Robert sent a humorous email about bumper stickers to his distribution list, a mixed group of family and friends, including church deacons and our pastor. Robert's forwarding comment was *This is great.*

I was horrified when I read the email that to me was anything but great. Among the 30 or so bumper stickers listed, only a couple caused me to even crack a smile. One slightly amusing sticker reminded me of our road trip experiences: *He Who Hesitates Not Only is Lost, but is Miles from The Next Exit.* The rest of the bumper stickers were crude, crass, and critical.

I replied to Robert's email at 9:52 p.m.: *I can't believe you sent this to people at church! Some of this is quite inappropriate. I think you should send a follow-up apology.*

I was horrified again when I realized that in my haste and at the late hour, I had used the *Reply All* feature. Everyone read what I intended as a private reply to Robert. The error was intensified by my saved signature paragraph quoting Scripture:

> *The wise in heart will be called understanding, And sweetness of speech increases persuasiveness.* ∞ *Proverbs 16:21*

My reply was not sweet and did not persuade Robert to send an apology. Instead, at 10:08 p.m., I sent a purposeful email to Robert's distribution list: *And now I need to apologize. I only intended to send this message to Robert!*

My dear friend, Lorrie, responded exactly when I needed to hear an encouraging word: *You and Robert are so precious to us! You have no idea how sweet you are, and how funny, and how precious!!! We love you two!!!!!!!! :)*

The Wedding Song and Twenty-Fifth Anniversary

In June 2006, we did some damage repair in our relationship when we attended the wedding of Ron and Jeanne. Robert took the opportunity to work on the promise he made to me when we first met—to take me to every state in the union. The wedding in Vermont brought us to a total of visiting 40 states together. The service was reminiscent of our

1981 Florida wedding when the musical reflection was Paul Stookey's "Wedding Song." It was a great three-day weekend enjoyed with many little people friends.

Two weeks later, we traveled to Milwaukee, Wisconsin for LPA's annual conference. Just as in 1982, when Robert was LPA president and we had worn our wedding clothes in the fashion show—the custom for couples who had married in the prior year—I was LPA president in 2006, and we wore the same wedding clothes in celebration of our 25th wedding anniversary—thanks to our success on the South Beach Diet that year! Although it was no longer customary for bridal couples to model their wedding clothes in the fashion show, we chose to end my presidency on a positive apolitical note.

In October, we continued our 25th anniversary celebration spending a four-day weekend in Nashville with Ray, who'd been a groomsman in our 1981 NZ wedding, and my Aunt Janet. We had a great weekend relaxing in their downtown apartment, dining in fun restaurants like the Wildhorse Saloon, enjoying the fall colors, riding Cumberland River on the General Jackson River Boat, touring the Cheekwood Botanical Garden and Museum of Art, and just generally being together.

I was happy that we bought a heart-shaped anniversary ring with a ruby to match the 10- and 20-year anniversary rings already on my left hand. Robert was happy that he worked in some recruiting of students with disabilities at Vanderbilt for Entry Point! Given Robert's predisposition to the unexpected, it was no surprise to learn that his visit probably caused the writing of an incident report.

Janet and I learned of Robert's predicament when he called to say his scooter had broken down, but not to worry he had called the police. It did not sound like a 911 emergency to us but, thankfully, Robert had only called campus police. He needed help getting the scooter to a public street where he could catch a cab back to the apartment. Here he enlisted the help of the building maintenance worker to dismantle the scooter and reconnect a loose wire. With hardly a minute to spare, Ray loaded our two scooters and luggage into the car for the ride to the airport. We softened our farewell blues with an emerging plan to reunite in Florida for Christmas 2006.

It was not possible for Janet and Ray to join us for the renewal of our wedding vows in a Sunday morning church service in October 2006.

Although I lacked the artistic flare of Nan and Kathleen who arranged the church wedding flowers 25 years earlier, I did the church flowers myself. I was amazed that my purchase of pink and purple carnations at the flea market filled three large vases.

At the end of the Sunday morning service, we walked the aisle together with the music director singing the "Wedding Song" and a slide presentation of our weddings in Papakura, New Zealand, and Hobe Sound, Florida. We may have fit into our original wedding clothes, but there was no fooling anyone that we were 25 years younger. The slides made the then and now contrast quite evident.

Both Robert's family and our church family witnessed the renewal of our wedding vows. When asked to renew my vow to stand by Robert no matter what happens, respecting his individuality, understanding his needs, accepting his changes and enjoying his love until death parts us, the congregation laughed when I answered, "I will and I have."

It was encouraging to receive a card from Robert's niece Juliette, our junior bridesmaid at the Florida wedding:

> *You can't know what a joy it is for me that you and Angela have remained faithful to one another all these years and faithful to the promises you made to God. In such a changing world—yours is a great example.*

Pastor Lee closed the service praying the same prayer used by Reverend Andrew in New Zealand: "Eternal God, the Spring of Life and Giver of spiritual grace; bless these our friends that, living together, they may fulfill the vows and covenant made between them. May they ever remain in perfect love and peace together according to Your Spirit in Jesus Christ our Lord."

The celebration continued with cake served after church in the courtyard gazebo. Family and closer friends came to the house for a luncheon and afternoon together. Robert and I stood ready to share the rest of our lives together, no matter what might happen.

That fall, when studying Joshua 6 and seeing how God used Joshua to bring down the walls of Jericho, I recorded the following prayer in my faith journal:

> *Lord Jesus, help me to see my marriage through eyes of faith, help me to remain silent and encircle the relationship in obedience, and wait for You to give the order of when to shout!*

Chapter 23
Aortic Valve Replacement

Diagnosis and Surgery Research

Who would have thought changing doctors would save my life? But in March 2012, my primary care doctor retired and my new doctor noticed that my heart murmur was *kind of loud.* A cardiologist first diagnosed moderate aortic stenosis, but six months later found severe aortic stenosis that required open-heart surgery to replace the aortic valve. *Really?* I felt fine and did not have the common symptoms of dizziness, low energy, swollen ankles, or heart palpitations. Yes, I often woke up tired or light-headed, but I attributed that to sleep apnea even though I used a C-Pap machine. As a little person with many joint anomalies, I always anticipated the possibility of orthopedic surgery, but heart surgery had never crossed my mind.

The cardiologist recommended aortic valve replacement (AVR) surgery within the next 6 to 12 months. Although not an emergency, each passing month put me in jeopardy for congestive heart failure and death. I walked out of the doctor's office wondering what God was doing. Yet I knew that He was in control:

> *I know the Lord is always with me. I will not be shaken, for He is right beside me.* ∞ *Psalm 16:8, NLT*

I held onto these promises and was already grateful for two things: first, the cardiologist recognized that I should not have the surgery in Stuart. And second, I had time to locate a medical center with expertise in both dwarfism and AVR surgery.

Because the LPA Medical Advisory Board does not have a cardiologist, I spent October 2012 researching AVR surgery, thoracic surgeons, anesthesiologists and hospitals. I looked at credentials, patient satisfaction, surgical outcomes, rankings, infection rates, and dwarfism experience. In reviewing national rankings, I chose Johns Hopkins hospital—in the top three for heart care—and Dr. John V. Conte in the top 1% of doctors for his specialty.[1] Not only did Dr. Conte answer my email on the same day it was received, he also called me the next day. He was friendly, answered all my questions and agreed to speak to my cardiologist in Stuart. It helped that the Greenberg Center for Skeletal Dysplasias, which specializes in dwarfism genetics and orthopedics, is also housed at Hopkins.

Insurance Coverage

My next move was to get insurance company approval to go out-of-network. To be sure that I did not make any mistakes that could put us into bankruptcy, I requested an insurance company case manager. It was extraordinary when the case manager reported a provision in our health insurance policy that put Hopkins in-network.

Never doubt God's mighty power to work in you and accomplish all this. He will achieve infinitely more than your greatest request, your most unbelievable dream, and exceed your wildest imagination! He will outdo them all, for his miraculous power constantly energizes you . . . ∞ Ephesians 3:20, TPT

This was the third time God used this Scripture in my life.

No special approval was needed and the surgery would be billed at the lower in-network rates. I saw this as confirmation of the decision to go to Hopkins.

Pre-Surgery Preparations

Now I began planning for surgery with Dr. Conte's office coordinator. The next step was for me to have a cardiac catheterization. Dr. Conte agreed for me to have this in Florida, but it took a whole month to satisfy the insurance company's pre-authorization requirement. With two cardiologists involved, which one should write the pre-authorization? Once this was resolved, Dr. Conte agreed for me to have the cardiac catheterization in January 2013 so that the diagnostic and surgery costs would both apply to my annual deductible in the same calendar year. However, given that I was now evidencing some cardiac symptoms, Dr. Conte cautioned me not to schedule any later.

Next, I added a prayer team to my medical team. I posted details of my diagnosis, cardiac catheterization and pending surgery on Facebook and the church prayer chain. I sought prayers for wisdom, skill, and patience for everyone involved, especially Robert, the surgical team, and the post-operative caregivers. I shared what I prayed before Robert's hip replacement surgeries in 1997:

Some trust in chariots and some in horses, but we trust in the name of the LORD our God. ∞ *Psalm 20:7, NIV*

The love, support, and prayer commitments were very encouraging. We were surprised when our friend Martha said Robert and I were two of her greatest heroes. Another friend said she would be storming heaven's gate. Someone else shared a favorite Scripture passage:

Don't worry about anything; instead, pray about everything. Tell God what you need, and thank Him for all He has done. Then you will experience God's peace, which exceeds anything we can understand. His peace will guard your hearts and minds as you live in Christ Jesus. ∞ *Philippians 4:6-7, NLT*

Our prayers were answered when the heart catheterization went very well. Robert was at my bedside before and after the procedure and helped me to clean up the two meals the hospital served. He was then so exhausted, he was the one to need a nap when we got home.

Dr. Aggarwal, the cardiac interventionist, advised that the AVR surgery should happen in the January/February 2013 timeframe. He did not tell me to get on the next plane, but he warned against delay. Dr. Conte agreed, but he threw a curveball when he asked if anyone had suggested a chest wall reconstruction to improve my lung function. Again, not something that had ever crossed my mind. He recommended discussing this with my pulmonologist.

Not wanting to stall setting a surgery date, I was grateful Dr. Charnvitayapong (Dr. C) scheduled a pulmonary function test with a respiratory therapist the next day. By the end of the week, Dr. C called to say that he did not see a need for a chest-wall reconstruction because the lung-function test looked normal for my size. He also discussed his findings with Dr. Conte who then cleared the way to schedule the AVR surgery on February 19, 2013.

CarePages Communication

Now we added a plan to communicate with friends and family around the world and across the US. We wanted people to get the same information, know how to pray, have an opportunity to post messages, and save us from the broken-record syndrome. We chose CarePages.[2]

One month prior to surgery I opened a CarePage called *angelaheartavr* and posted a link on Facebook. I shared my story and invited people to the web page for updates on the preparation, heart surgery, and recovery. In my first post, I wrote in part:

> *The best way people can support me is to pray to our Great Physician through His Son, the Lord Jesus Christ . . . I love the imagery in Psalm 91 and the first part of verse 4, "He will cover you with his feathers, and under His wings you will find refuge;" [NIV] . . . Please pray that Robert and I will be faithful in honoring God through this painful process.*

Final Preparations for Surgery

So began the countdown to complete work tasks before going on medical leave for six to eight weeks. At the same time, I resisted the temptation to say I was too busy to begin the weekly Bible study by Beth Moore, *Breaking Free*. Even though I could only attend three studies before going to Johns Hopkins in Baltimore, the timing was perfect.

As Beth Moore said, "We will find freedom to the degree our hearts accept, rely, and respond to the truth of God's Word."[3]

God wanted me to respond by trusting Him to heal my heart physically and spiritually. In week two, I wrote this prayer:

> *Dear Lord my Savior and King, please touch my heart to be soft and pliable in Your Hands so that I am willing to do everything You have planned for me. Please help me through the AVR so that my physical heart will continue to pump blood through my body so that I am able to serve You and glorify You for the days You have numbered for me on earth. Amen.*

Two days later, I received final surgery instructions to report to the Johns Hopkins Outpatient Center for pre-admission testing the day before surgery. But I freaked over one appalling paragraph highlighted in yellow. I needed a written statement from my dentist on the condition of my teeth. This was necessary to avoid any gum or tooth infections settling in the valve. If only I had been more diligent about going to the dentist.

This was one of those times and situations when I prayed a specific Scripture, asking for His peace:

Now may the Lord of peace Himself continually grant you peace in every circumstance. ∞ 2 Thessalonians 3:16a

When I feared postponement of the surgery, Beth Moore reminded me to trust God and fix my thoughts on Him. So, I trusted God and He got me a dental appointment in a couple of days instead of a couple of months. I trusted God again when the dentist declined to write the letter clearing me for surgery, but referred me for a same day appointment with a periodontist. I knew God's peace when the periodontist wrote the letter to Dr. Conte—after a thorough debridement and cleaning of my teeth.

Finally, on February 12, 2013, I received written approval from my insurance provider for the AVR surgery and five days hospitalization. Now it was like getting ready for an extended vacation without the anticipation of fun and games. I got a haircut, paid my credit card balance, and stopped the mail. In the event that this was a one-way trip, I also updated my Last Will and Testament, named Robert as my health-care proxy and added his name to my bank account.

In my February 14th Bible study, Beth Moore gave me this gem:

Prayer matters. The Spirit of God released through our prayers and the prayers of others turn cowards into conquerors, chaos into calm, cries into comfort.[4]

She had this on good authority given Paul's words:

I also pray that you will understand the incredible greatness of God's power for us who believe Him. This is the same mighty power that raised Christ from the dead and seated Him in the place of honor at God's right hand in the heavenly realms. ∞ Ephesians 1:19-20, NLT

On February 16, 2013, we flew to Baltimore confident in the power of God and the many prayers offered on our behalf. Given that it was winter, we built in an extra day to avoid any stress caused by potential weather delays. The trip was stress-free and we enjoyed our extra day at the Baltimore aquarium with Paula, niece Juliette, and family.

The February 18th pre-op appointments went well until I met Dr. Conte's physician's assistant. He was on the verge of stopping the surgery because of my dripping nose. He had to be convinced that it was not a cold but my response to an over 30° drop in temperature from Stuart to Baltimore. Thankfully, he was persuaded and found me fit for surgery.

Informed Decisions with Dr. Conte

In the afternoon, we met Dr. Conte for the first time. It was surreal when Robert and I sat across the desk from him discussing whether to implant a mechanical or biologic (pig or cow tissue) aortic valve. This was no longer research. I was now the subject and the next day I would become a data point in medical research.

In choosing what type of aortic valve to implant, Dr. Conte boiled it down to two options:

(1) The biologic does not need blood-thinning medication but wears out and requires a reoperation for replacement in about 10 years;

(2) The mechanical does require blood-thinning medication but should last the rest of my life.

Although avoidance of a reoperation was the most appealing thing about a mechanical valve, I asked about the risk of reoperation to replace a defective mechanical valve. Dr. Conte was dismissive of my concern, until I mentioned reading about aortic valve recalls between 1979 and 1986. He assured me that manufacturer defects and recalls were no longer an issue and held up an encased sample sitting on his desk.

Dr. Conte had a very different concern—I would forget my post-surgery imperative not to lift more than five pounds for at least six weeks. He knew how hard this would be given that daily living activities like getting on and off a chair or toilet and in and out of bed involved me lifting my entire body-weight of 72 pounds. One body lift could cause my rib cage to go out of alignment as indicated by a grinding sensation. Now it was my turn to reassure Dr. Conte that I was highly motivated not to have a repeat surgery and that Robert's rehabilitation engineering skills would fill that need perfectly.

As to the aortic valve choice, I had to put aside my fears and trust the judgment of the doctor God had led me to. We accepted Dr. Conte's recommendation to implant the Carbomedics Top Hat aortic mechanical valve. I was always partial to wearing hats, but only God would see this one.

Day of Surgery

Robert and Paula accompanied me when I reported for surgery at 9 a.m. on February 19, 2013. After doing everything that was asked of me the night before—eating a light evening meal, applying an antiseptic agent to my skin, and having no food or liquid since midnight—I was ready. Naturally, I would rather have been somewhere else, but I was at peace having entrusted God with the outcome.

When the surgery time lagged, I could easily have lapsed into worry. The surgery involved splitting open my breastbone, stopping my heart and hooking it up to a heart-lung machine, replacing the damaged aortic valve with my new Top Hat valve, restarting my heart, and adding temporary pacemaker wires to help maintain a normal heart rhythm. The surgical dangers could also have flooded my mind—bleeding, blood clots, irregular heart rhythm, infection, kidney problems, a stroke, or death. Instead of filling my mind with these thoughts, I used my phone to read various Psalms aloud to Robert and Paula.

After being wheeled into the assembly line in the pre-op area, I was asked what kind of surgery I was having.

I said, "I am having an aortic valve replacement with a Carbomedics Top Hat mechanical valve."

I probably would have said more, but the inquirer interrupted me and said, "Most people just say 'heart surgery.'"

I guess he was only checking that I was correctly tagged for the cardiac operating room (OR).

It is a good thing the basics are checked, because when Dr. Rosanne (Rosie) Sheinberg, my anesthesiologist, came to meet me she immediately realized that I did not have achondroplasia which had been mistakenly recorded in my chart. We discussed the limited range of motion in my neck that would make intubation difficult. If done wrong, she could cut off my airway with fatal consequences. Therefore, Dr. Rosie warned that she might intubate me while I was awake to get accurate feedback on how I was tolerating the intubation tube. It sounded traumatic, but I was grateful that she was conscientious about not ending the surgery before it began. It was another confirmation that coming to Hopkins was the right decision.

During the six hours I was in the OR and recovery, Nurse Sandra called Robert and Paula several times with progress reports. After the surgery, Dr. Conte talked to them in the waiting room and said it went as well as expected. He mentioned that my airway restriction did not allow him to put a camera down my airway to check for any life-threatening air bubbles in my heart; instead, he squeezed my heart with his hands to be sure no bubbles remained. Yet another confirmation that coming to Hopkins was the right decision.

Robert and Paula visited me briefly in the ICU before returning to the hotel. Robert says he choked up seeing me connected to nine monitors, five bags on intravenous poles, and four drainage containers. The nurse assured them I was in good hands.

ICU Monitoring and Following Instructions

By the time Robert and Paula returned the next morning, I was alert, the intubation tube was out, and I was asking for water and my glasses. When staff sat me up, I was talking a mile a minute. Paula had to stop me because Dr. Conte was standing at the door. He said I reminded him of his wife and declared Robert a saint. Paula wrote on CarePages that "Saint" Robert had failed to post a surgery report the night before. Robert's defense was that the cell phone batteries died by 5:00 p.m., he got back to the hotel late, and was too tired and mentally drained to post anything.

On the surgical rounds, the floor doctor chided the interns for overdosing me with Lasix, a drug to limit fluid accumulation and swelling of the body. Then, the doctor was put in his place when his plan to put a camera down my throat was nixed. Instead, he followed an instruction to put a *difficult airway* band on my wrist. But the scariest thing was when the resident assigned to remove several drainage tubes going directly into my heart was teaching another resident how to do it. I was told there would be dire consequences if I took a breath during the process. It was the longest 60 seconds I can ever remember as the resident kept pausing to explain each step.

After being transferred to the progressive care unit, I diligently followed sternal precautions with regard to lifting, pulling, pushing, coughing, or straining. There was no way I was going to forget. The oxygen cannula in my nose, the gripping sensation in my throat, the heart monitor in my pocket, the IV in my hand, and incision in my chest were all excellent reminders. This meant I had to depend on staff to lift me in and out of bed and on and off a chair. Thankfully, the successful search for an adjustable-height commode gave me independence in one respect.

I advanced my recovery by frequent breathing exercises and walking two or three times a day accompanied by a nurse to help with my IV pole and portable oxygen tank. My hospital gown was shortened with safety pins to avoid an accidental fall. One nurse on the floor saw the indignity of my garb and gave me not one but two pairs of pajamas.

Prayer and Support

Two days after surgery, Tropical Farms Baptist Church in Stuart blessed me with a garden dish of small plants. It was great to know they were remembering me in prayer. This was also the day Dr. Rosie, my anesthesiologist, came to check if I remembered being intubated while still awake. She was happy to hear that I did not. We also discussed how all through the surgery she was involved in calculating the quantity of fluids and drugs put into my body. I learned that she was on an integrated medicine fellowship when she asked to interview me about how I prepared for such a big surgery. I was more than happy to help.

Dr. Rosie returned the next day to ask about the source of my strength and for advice on how to improve the patient/physician relationship. I shared that God is my refuge and strength and that I was being held up in prayer by many believers and supported by friends and family on CarePages. She was touched by the image of women in my Bible study group encircling and praying for me before I left for Baltimore.

In a later review of the 47 get-well cards received, I noted that prayer was the most-used word and God was the second most-used word. He sustained me through this ordeal and coming lifestyle changes.

> *The Lord is my rock, my fortress, and my Savior; my God is my rock, in whom I find protection. He is my shield, the power that saves me, and my place of safety.* ∞ *Psalm 18:2, NLT*

One clear answer to prayer was not feeling like I had been run over by a bus, as many people report after open-heart surgery. I was acutely aware of the hit to my body, but experienced very little pain. After a couple of days, I told the nurse I did not need the oxycodone pain pill and switched to Tylenol PM at night.

Getting comfortable in bed was difficult. One night I had to call the nurse because I was having trouble breathing. It felt like I was going to die. The nurse assured me that this was common and sat with me until my respiration improved. She also repositioned the pillows at my back and turned up the oxygen level. I praised God for nursing expertise and compassion. This is a role they share with God:

The Lord nurses them when they are sick and restores them to health.
    ∞ *Psalm 41:3, NLT*

My daytime nurse was surprised I had so many visitors given that I was from out of town. Of course, she expected to see my two companions, Saint Robert and sister-in-law Paula, but there were several others. Two visitors came from the Hopkins Greenberg Center for Skeletal Dysplasias—the director, Dr. Julie Hoover Fong, and the clinical program coordinator, Colleen Gioffreda; a cousin from Maryland and church friends en route to Rochester, New York. In her second visit, Dr. Julie told me that Dr. Conte was highly regarded among his peers and was the surgeon doctors chose when they needed heart surgery. She also shared that he had double-wired my rib cage when putting me back together to prevent any movement long after there were no sternal precautions.

Discharge Planning and Hospital Release

During my discharge planning, Dr. Conte stated I was ready to go to a local rehabilitation center. I reminded him that he had previously agreed that I could rehab at home in Stuart. Thankfully, the occupational therapist (OT) was conducting her inpatient evaluation when Dr. Conte said this. She asked him to hold his decision until after her evaluation. It was a huge relief when Dr. Conte accepted the OT recommendation for in-home rehabilitation.

Six days after surgery, I was discharged from the hospital to our hotel for a few days of outpatient monitoring. Unfortunately, the discharge did not go smoothly because a float nurse who was unfamiliar with the hospital handled the paperwork and prescriptions. She sent my prescriptions to one of the five Hopkins pharmacies—and carelessly directed us to the wrong one. When we discovered the error, it was late in the afternoon with limited time before the pharmacy closed. Worse yet, the pharmacy with my prescription was in another building that involved going outside in the 30° temperature and falling snow. Needless to say, we were quite distressed. Thankfully, Paula came to the rescue, braved the weather, and made it to the pharmacy just in time.

Meanwhile we were concerned that Mohammed, the owner of our hotel car service, was waiting for us. Paula and Robert had found him to be friendly and helpful on their daily shuttles to and from their hospital visits with me. We need not have worried that Mohammed would leave us stranded. He greeted us warmly and safely lifted me into his vehicle. Then he drove us to another part of the hospital where Paula waited with the prescriptions.

The welcome reception we received upon my return to the Sheraton Baltimore City Center hotel was like coming home to family. The business travel sales manager, Kimberly Lansaw, had given us a discounted hospital rate and instructed engineering staff to make access accommodations in our room, such as removing the closer on the heavy door and removing a mattress to lower the bed. All of the staff genuinely cared about my medical progress and encouraged Robert coming and going from his daily hospital visits.

The manager even emailed us at home:

I hope all is going well and that Mrs. Angela is feeling well. Please send her my thoughts and let her know everyone here is asking about the two of you. Our staff really misses your family.

It was an easy decision to write a favorable review on the hotel website. To this day we remember the kindness of Manager Kimberly, Cliff at the bell station, and our driver, Mohammed.

After hospital discharge, we had three more days in Baltimore before returning to Florida. One day we rode the accessible downtown buses, scootering to a museum and a lovely restaurant.

Outpatient meal with my faithful caregivers, Paula & Robert

The other two days were outpatient appointments, including one with Dr. Conte. He was relaxed and friendly which gave us hope he would agree for me to fly home on March 1st. However, he would only let me go on the condition that a companion travel with us to lift me as needed. Paula was in the waiting room and accepted the assignment even though she had planned to spend more time with her daughter, Juliette, and family in Virginia. Dr. Conte confirmed how much he cared when he asked us to let him know when we arrived home safely.

Traveling Home to Stuart

Seating in the bulkhead row made our flight home easier. However, the flight was not without incident. When Paula stepped past Robert to help me get more comfortable in my seat, she asked him to hold her tomato juice. She did not know that Robert was only wearing one hearing aid and did not hear her. She let go the drink and Robert took a tomato juice shower.

It was not until we arrived at Palm Beach International (PBI) airport that Paula and I learned that Robert had misplaced his second hearing aid. Apparently, someone in Baltimore noticed that Robert had left it on the scooter seat and stored it, so upon our arrival, the baggage staff delivered two scooters and one hearing aid.

We were very aware of God's hand on our entire trip. Mohammed had taken us to the Baltimore/Washington International airport when our pre-reserved ride did not show up. At the PBI airport, cousin Gary met us in Robert's van with room for all our stuff and the running board that made it easier to lift me into the vehicle. And no words could cover the sacrifice Paula made to share her spiritual gifts of helping, serving, and mercy for Robert and myself during our time in and return from Baltimore.

Every time I think of you, I give thanks to my God.
∞ *Philippians 1:3, NLT*

Cardiac Care Transferred Back to Florida

After returning from Baltimore, my cardiac care transferred to Dr. Aggarwal in Palm Beach Gardens. At my first visit three days after coming home, he was all smiles until my international normalized ratio (INR) test revealed my blood thickness at about one. This put me way below the therapeutic level between two and three and made my blood too thick and prone to blood clots forming in the aortic valve. If the INR level gets above three, the blood becomes too thin and susceptible to internal bleeding. But in my case, regulating the Coumadin dose was harder than anticipated—my INR was nontherapeutic about 24% of the time in 2013. Instead of testing monthly, as I was told before surgery, I started out testing every few days and eventually settled into testing weekly.

My first INR tests were at my cardiologist office, then at the laboratory, and in July I received a home INR test kit. Whenever I received a nontherapeutic INR test result, Dr. Aggarwal's nurse called to tell me whether to increase or decrease my Coumadin dose or vitamin K intake.

At Johns Hopkins we had received training with a pharmacist on how vitamin K interacts with Coumadin and were given a chart showing the amount of vitamin K in different foods. I was told I could eat whatever I liked, provided I was consistent with vitamin K intake. This did not work out for me. I couldn't eat high vitamin-K vegetables like broccoli, brussels sprouts, and spinach and was limited to low vitamin-K fruit and vegetables like avocado, blueberries, cauliflower, grapes and peas. I hate being a picky eater, but this was a lifestyle change I had to accept.

The need for God's patience and strength continued along with my dependence on His Word.

God blesses those who patiently endure testing and temptation. Afterward they will receive the crown of life that God has promised to those who love Him. ∞ *James 1:12, NL T*

But the reason we can persevere is because of the consistent nature of our Creator:

Have you never heard? Have you never understood? The Lord is the everlasting God, the Creator of all the earth. He never grows weak or weary. No one can measure the depths of His understanding. He gives power to the weak and strength to the powerless. ∞ *Isaiah 40:28b-29, NLT*

So be truly glad. There is wonderful joy ahead, even though you must endure many trials for a little while. These trials will show that your faith is genuine. It is being tested as fire tests and purifies gold—though your faith is far more precious than mere gold. So when your faith remains strong through many trials, it will bring you much praise and glory and honor on the day when Jesus Christ is revealed to the whole world. ∞1 Peter 1:6-7, NLT

Many of these Scriptures came to mind in March 2013 when I returned to my *Breaking Free* Bible study.

Home Adaptations and Therapy

Although approved for four registered nurse home visits, the only one used was for the initial clinical assessment. However, I used all six of the approved physical therapy (PT) home visits. PT Dave was very adept at modifying his exercise regime to my orthopedic limitations. He taught

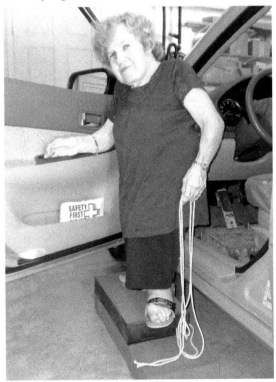

me how to stay physically active without breaching sternal precautions.

As anticipated upon returning home, Robert's rehabilitation engineering skills helped me get in and out of bed—and a vehicle—without lifting or pulling. He placed custom low-rise steps next to the bed and used incredibly light-weight closed-cell foam to make two steps for getting in and out of the car. He attached a long string to the steps so I could pull the steps in after me. This was right up Robert's alley.

Steps save lifting my 70 pounds into the car

However, Robert quickly tired of his duties as chauffeur, personal shopper, and laundry guy. He tried to get out of folding clothes and asked why I couldn't do it. He forgot that sternal precautions included no exaggerated arm movements. Robert was relieved that we had a housekeeping service every two weeks that saved him from the rigor of sweeping, mopping, cleaning, or vacuuming. He was almost free from cooking duties by dear friends who brought enough meals to feed us for a month.

I am thankful to Robert for loving and caring for me through such a difficult time.

Then the Lord God said, "It is not good for the man to be alone. I will make a helper who is just right for him." ∞ Genesis 2:18, NLT

As the Beth Moore study continued into April, I was reminded that God insists on pushing us beyond our human limitations so that we understand the Source of our power.

We are like common clay jars that carry this glorious treasure within, so that the extraordinary overflow of power will be seen as God's, not ours. ∞ 2 Corinthians 4:7, TPT

Cleared to Return to Work

Six weeks after surgery I received clearance to return to work part-time. Six months earlier God had anticipated my need for light duty and moved my office from a business center back to our home. This eliminated the commute and made it easier for me to ease back into work. It's incredible how God provided, long before the need was even apparent to me.

When I returned to work full-time and was cleared to drive eight weeks after surgery, I discontinued the CarePages updates. During the three months my CarePage was active, my 146 supporters had a huge role in my recovery. I had posted 78 updates and received 799 encouraging messages and prayers.

One Year Later

One year after my AVR, the flowers were blooming, my electrocardiogram was boring, and my echocardiogram was very good.

Give thanks to the Lord, for He is good! ∞ 1 Chronicles 16:34a, NLT

My eternal gratitude goes to the Lord my God, Robert and Paula, family and friends, and medical partners who helped me through the deep waters. All credit for my recovery without complications goes to God Who graciously responded to the many prayers offered on my behalf.

Chapter 24
Dad's Alzheimer's Disease

Faith and Finances

For many years my father reported getting out of bed, throwing back the curtains and saying, "Good morning, Lord." When the morning was not so bright, he would laugh and say, "Lord, You'll have to do a bit better than that!" And He did.

Dad's faith is what kept him going during the setbacks that delayed his retirement. His finances took a serious hit when he divorced at age 68; he was sued by a disgruntled real estate buyer at age 69; and both knees were replaced at age 71. In addition, Dad's plan to turn things around by flipping an investment property failed—instead his investment became a financial burden, not a retirement nest egg.

Something Was Wrong with Dad

Dad wrote in his notebook filled with random thoughts and reminders, "I am definitely ready to stop work. . . I feel I am no longer sharp enough to carry on in real estate." He described himself as muddled, mixed up, and not working properly.

Robert and I did not need to read the notations in Dad's notebook to know he had a problem. He would call in the early hours of the morning just to tell us how much he enjoyed looking at the stars from the beach-house balcony. Dad was not just confused about the 18-hour time difference between New Zealand and Florida, but he also didn't care that he was waking us from a deep sleep. After receiving several such calls, we turned the ringer off in the bedroom and let the calls go to voicemail. For Dad's next birthday, his three kids and spouses chipped in to buy him a telescope hoping to enhance his stargazing and eliminate the early, early wake up calls.

Whangamata Residence and Sydney Vacations

Despite our doubts about Dad's readiness to live alone at the beach house, he retired and moved to Whangamata in May 2007. Even so, in the first few months he regularly drove the 90 miles to and from Papakura. After living there for 52 years he had a hard time letting old ties go. We encouraged Dad to connect with a church in Whangamata, but in retrospect, we realize he was unable to start over with new people in a new church.

In August 2007, Deborah persuaded Dad to come to Sydney for two weeks to surprise Greg on his birthday. She was also planting the seed that Sydney was the better place for Dad to live. But as much as Dad loved his family, he was not ready to give up his independence. Respecting his decision, Deborah and Greg both returned with Dad to Whangamata to help him make the top story of the beach house into his home.

The good news was that Dad's former personal assistant in the real estate business moved to Whangamata a few months after Dad. Sue and her husband Terry rented the downstairs unit year-round. This helped everyone—the rental income covered the property expenses and gave Dad friends who looked out for his well-being.

Although we were aware that Dad was forgetful, we had no idea how a houseful of people would stress him. In December 2007, the whole family was home for Deborah's 50th birthday. Dad enjoyed having us all under one roof but was overwhelmed with the activity, and his pet peeves—lights left on, wet towels on the bathroom floor, and clothes not put away—were in overdrive.

Thankfully, this did not stop us enjoying the celebration of Deborah's birthday or Christmas. We each contributed one gift to a grab bag, but we made sure Dad got the one Deborah had earmarked for him—a porcelain white-bearded Santa sitting in a beach chair with an umbrella, wearing a beach hat, shorts, flip flops (jandals), and red jacket. Dad regularly answered the phone, "Santa speaking," so this was the perfect gift for him. The family all enjoyed a good laugh as Dad held Santa up for everyone to see.

Even when Dad was working and living in Papakura, for several years he rented out the top unit at Whangamata at premium summer rates for about six weeks. Now that Dad lived at the beach house, he continued this practice in December and January by staying with the family in Sydney. In January 2009, Robert and I came from Florida so that my whole family could be together.

The photos posted on Facebook gave no hint of anything amiss with Dad. There were happy pictures of our New South Wales visits to Hunter Valley and the Chocolate Factory, the Blue Mountains, and the Rocks in

Sydney. The untold stories were heartbreaking:

Dad refused to get out of the car to admire the Three Sisters rock formation at the Blue Mountains saying, "I've been around the world and have seen enough scenery in my time."

He threw his drink in Greg's face at a restaurant when he disagreed with what Greg said, leaving the table in a huff saying he would walk home. Besides being too far, Dad had no idea where he was. When Greg followed Dad, he found him standing on the sidewalk just around the corner. Dad returned to the table with Greg like nothing had happened.

The time had come to get a better handle on what was wrong. Dad agreed to have Deborah's doctor give him a routine medical examination. Blood work and a brain scan did not show any physical reason for Dad's memory loss. The recommendation was for Dad to consult with a geriatrician for cognitive/mental testing. Regrettably this could not be scheduled before Dad returned to Whangamata in February.

All three children and spouses did our best to monitor Dad's situation from afar via Skype and the phone. And we had reason to be concerned. For example, Dad lost his way driving his Whangamata neighbor to Hamilton—the town Dad grew up in and once knew like the back of his hand. His brother, Stew, and sister-in-law Joye had expected Dad for dinner, but his call asking for help didn't come until about 10:00 p.m. Uncle Stew found him on the outskirts of Hamilton and Dad followed him back to their house.

Dad's Move to Sydney

My brother, Greg, and his wife, Julie, used Dad's birthday on May 28, 2009 as a pretext to visit him in Whangamata, but they were primarily there to assess his situation. Several people approached them on the side to report that Dad was not doing well. Greg convinced Dad to come back to Sydney with them for a holiday, while we privately thought this trip to Sydney would be the one to change Dad's residence.

As Dad later described it in a 2010 letter to extended family and friends that I scribed for him:

I left New Zealand in June 2009 and returned with Deborah and Julie for a week in September 2009 to pack my things and say goodbye to as many people as possible. I often talk about needing to get back to New Zealand, but I don't have any immediate plans. I have two homes here:

one with Deborah, Rob, and Ashley; and the other with Greg, Julie, and Sam. I am part of the sandwich generation—I am the top slice; Greg and Julie, and Deborah and Rob are the filling; and Ashley and Sam are the bottom slice. (It is ironic that I still come out on top.) . . . Some days, I don't even remember where I live. I feel like I am away with the fairies.

At Deborah's house, I have one whole wall covered with family photographs. I do my best to show this off to visitors. They don't know who you all are, but I make sure to tell them. When I go to Greg's house, I bring my digital photo frame that has over 300 family photos. . . I also enjoy going through my box of photos dating back to my childhood dancing days.

Dad's move to Sydney was a tough transition for everyone. For several months, we methodically worked with Sue, Dad's former personal assistant, to sort through accounts that needed to be paid, transferred, or cancelled. All went smoothly until it came to the renewal of Dad's NZ Automobile Association (AA) membership. I recommended cancellation and saw renewal as a pointless, sentimental waste of money because Dad was no longer driving or living in New Zealand. But Sue knew how proud Dad was of his 50-plus-year AA membership and Deborah knew he felt like everything he knew had been taken away from him. Once I had all the facts, I agreed that renewing his AA card might help to cheer up Dad.

Our family hoped that with a healthy diet and more encouragement, Dad would eat less and exercise more. Yet he lacked motivation, resisted going for walks, and ate too much. When Deborah went to work in the morning, she laid out food for the day on the counter—morning and afternoon snacks and a sandwich for lunch. One day when she came home mid-morning, she found that Dad had already eaten the food laid out for him.

Deborah said, "He is an adult and I can't boss him around too much or he will get the sh*ts."

After a few months, all three siblings agreed that Sydney should be Dad's permanent residence. We also committed to consensus on any future decisions involving Dad. Once a decision was made, we divvied up the action items. Greg and Deborah had the lion's share of the work in the day-to-day care of Dad. Greg exercised Dad's enduring power of attorney (POA) on legal and financial matters. As the holder of Dad's POA for health and welfare decisions, Deborah handled the voluminous paperwork and bureaucracy related to applications for Australian residency, Medicare, and transfer of Dad's NZ pension to Australia. The best I could do was handle the NZ bills via online banking, listen and encourage, pray, and visit every year instead of every other year. Thankfully, Robert agreed to this extra expense as part of our marriage commitment: "for better or worse."

Dementia Symptoms Increase

Since we had no way of knowing how many more birthdays dad would enjoy, I flew to Sydney for Dad's 76th birthday in May 2010. In his 2010 letter he described his birthday dinner party this way:

I am now 38 on each foot. Sam took a picture of my bare feet one day and emailed it to Deborah. She printed it out and there was the photo on my dinner plate. I thought the feet looked familiar. The house was nicely decorated with balloons and streamers. Everyone was surprised that I was not surprised that Angela was there for my birthday dinner. Why would I be surprised that my daughter would come to wish me happy birthday? I kept asking her where Robert was. She kept telling me he was in Florida.

In the three weeks I was in Sydney, I could see firsthand how Dad's undiagnosed dementia was advancing. Not only was he unaware of travel distance, he was easily confused. At Greg's place, one of Dad's daily activities was going to the mailbox. Dad would handle every envelope repeatedly looking for one with his name on it. Since Greg, Julie, and Sam all had the same last name as Dad, he regularly opened their mail. They often had to hunt in his room for their missing mail and did their best to beat Dad to the mailbox.

Dad was also getting confused with the monthly rotation between Greg and Deborah's house. One doctor—who lacked a grip on how the world works—even suggested that Dad stay put in one house and that the two families do the switching.

Dad had also lost the social skill of sharing. I witnessed this when Dad and I spent the day with Deborah who was managing a Sydney-wide Dance School competition. We accepted the invitation to join the volunteers for afternoon tea. A delicious homemade cake was offered, to share among several volunteers—but there was not enough for seconds. Dad got upset when Deborah and I intercepted his hand reaching out for another piece. When he and I went out for lunch with Greg—a substantial meal—we ordered one piece of rhubarb cake to share. The waitress put the cake down in front of Dad who claimed full possession of the whole piece. Not a battle worth fighting.

Agitation was another constant, especially when Dad tried to remember what he had forgotten. He said, "I am not the happy-go-lucky person I used to be."

Dad was very restless and always on the move looking for something. If he remembered what he was looking for, he usually didn't find it. At this point, he even needed reminders to shower and change his clothes.

Medical Diagnosis

In his 2010 letter Dad wrote about the danger of forgetfulness:

This year I was diagnosed with Alzheimer's . . . This would explain why I have trouble remembering things . . . let me warn you about Ashley's cat. Millie only likes being patted on the head. Don't even think about stroking her on the back. Even though Deborah keeps reminding me, I sometimes forget and have the scratches to show for it. Sam's dog, Matilda, and I get along much better. Greg even found Matilda alone in my bedroom one day with the door closed. I'm not sure how that happened.

Being with Dad for any extended time was exhausting and required lots of patience, a virtue Dad used to say "is seldom possessed by a woman and never by a man." He told the same stories over and over and over. It helped that he had lots of visitors in 2010 to listen to his stories. Despite the distance, family came to see Dad from Queensland, Australia; New Zealand; the United Kingdom; and the USA.

Dad's grandson, Sam, created a *Neil Muir Appreciation Group* on Facebook, a public group for people to post greetings, photos and memories of Dad. Sam called Dad "the legend."

Reverend Jeff New at Papakura East Presbyterian Church joined the group immediately:

My family have much to thank you for all your expertise in real estate, and helping us arrive at Papakura East and ministry here. You are indeed a legend. We thank God for you!

Our family had a lot of fun using Dad's group to record his sayings. A few are listed below:

I'm the tall dark handsome one.

They used to call me Twinkle Toes Muir.

(a reference to Dad's dancing and rugby league days)

Civility hurts no one.

I'm seldom right, but I'm never wrong.

If someone gives you trouble, kick them in the shins and climb up the bumps. (Dad's advice to me as a child)

There are only 364 days until Christmas.

(what Dad would say—every year—on December 26th)

After two years living with Greg and Deborah, leaving Dad home alone while the family went out to work or school was no longer safe. One day at Greg's place, Dad went through all the cupboards and opened every box of dried food looking for something to eat. He satisfied himself by eating "cookies" he found on the counter—they were dog biscuits.

Twenty-four/Seven Care Needed

Since Dad wasn't a cook, we never worried about dangers in the kitchen. Until we were proved wrong. Greg left a frozen pizza on the counter, turned on the oven and left the room until it reached baking temperature. Greg came back and found the pizza on fire. Dad had put the pizza in the oven without removing it from the box.

There were also safety challenges at Deborah's place. She came home from work on a cold wintry day to find Dad shivering on the back patio. He had locked himself out of the house and had been outside most of the day.

Lack of sleep took the greatest toll on Deborah. Dad would be up and down all night going to the bathroom. As a very light sleeper, Deborah heard his every move. Sometimes she had to get up to guide him to the bathroom or back to his bedroom. When a geriatric social worker heard all that was happening with Dad, she agreed the disease had progressed to the point where he needed round-the-clock care.

Residence at Alexander Aged Care

A miracle occurred when God provided a respected church-run facility currently advertising for residents in a new wing with a 50% discount on the bond. Alexander Aged Care had a private room/bathroom and made the commitment residents could keep the assigned room throughout their entire time in care. In other words, as Dad's medical needs increased, care would come to him rather than Dad being moved to a different wing.

Dad was included in the site visit and was happy and relaxed in the surroundings. The facility was also well-situated for Dad to have regular visitors.

The move to Alexander Aged Care triggered a new round of bureaucracy. Deborah waded through the paperwork to apply for institutional Medicare. Once again, Dad's finances were scrutinized— this time to determine the dollar amount of the nursing home bond. We then raised a mortgage on the Whangamata beach house to cover the cost.

The timing of Robert's and my Sydney visit in July 2011 was perfect. I was able to tour the Alexander Aged Care facility and read the contract before a final decision was made. Also, I helped select furniture for Dad's room and was pleased to be there on July 23rd when Dad moved into his new residence.

As the first resident in the new wing, Dad could pick any room he wanted. We chose a room close to the dining room so he would not have far to walk and hung his photo on the outside of his door to help him find his way back. Dad's room was cheerful with plenty of natural light and attractive curtains. We furnished it with his family photo collage, Santa ornament, comfortable guest chairs and a reclining armchair for Dad.

All three siblings and spouses went with Dad on his move-in day. Instead of a somber scene, it made for a nice family gathering. Dad was warmly greeted by friendly staff and was all smiles when he was served a delicious three-course meal.

We handled it like any other day and left Dad saying, "We'll see you later."

For Robert and me, it would be a lot later. After leaving Dad, we traveled to Port Douglas on the Great Barrier Reef before departing to

Florida from Brisbane. I would not see Dad for another year. Deborah and Greg would see Dad in a week after taking a much-needed break with us in Port Douglas. Dad's sister-in-law Janet and daughter-in-law, Julie, visited him while we were away to be sure he settled in well.

Port Douglas was just what the doctor ordered. We enjoyed a week together with no responsibilities surrounded by the beauty of God's creation in wildlife parks, the Daintree Rainforest, and on the Great Barrier Coral Reef. We held a parrot, cockatiels, and a koala so big that it hardly fit on Robert's lap.

When Robert was unable to manage a scuba-diving oxygen tank, Deborah reluctantly descended about 12 feet with him; both were donned in glass diver helmets attached to an oxygen hose. They marveled at fish swimming right past their faces. I was content to view the fish and coral from a glass-bottom submarine. Our encounter

It's a koala so no bear hugs today

with crocodiles occurred in the wild, but thankfully we were on a boat.

Dad quickly settled into Alexander Aged Care where he was comfortable, content, and enjoyed the food immensely. Despite our best effort, Dad often walked right past his photo hanging on his door. When he wandered into the wrong room, he sometimes shelved a personal item in there. When his electric razor was given up for lost, a new one was bought just before the original was found in another resident's room.

Dad had regular visitors as three out of four Sydney family members lived within five or ten minutes. Deborah stopped in on her way to work to help him shower, dress, and have breakfast. Janet visited most afternoons, often bringing him chocolate treats. Nathan, Dad's nephew, lived within walking distance and often visited with his two-year-old son, Logan, who gave Dad many kisses. Logan generally amused Dad with antics such as getting himself stuck in the chair beside Dad, wandering around with the warning sign for wet floors, and running around on the patio. Many photos show Logan and Dad together: Logan sitting on Dad's knee turning pages in a picture storybook while Dad smiled at him; Dad watching Logan intently do something cute; and Dad clapping hands with Logan.

In February 2012, we were shocked by Deborah's Facebook post of Dad with the shortest haircut we had ever seen on him. His beautiful head of silver hair had been scalped. The institutional care mentality—*it's easier to manage*—had taken one more piece of Dad's unique personhood from him.

Gradual Social Withdrawal

Dad had always been competitive, and was definitely in the running as the most-photographed man in Sydney. Naturally, we always asked Dad to smile for the camera. Before his Alzheimer's diagnosis, Dad had a cheerful and engaging personality. Yet the declining quality and frequency of his smile through the years was another marker of Dad's gradual withdrawal into himself. In January 2012, he was alert and could enjoy a meal at his assigned table in the dining room with a ready and natural smile for the camera. By September, we settled for a thumbs-up gesture after he opened his Father's Day gifts. Even so, a smile came easily the day Dad lived up to his reputation as a ladies' man. His afternoon tea guests included eight significant women in his life—daughters Angela and Deborah, daughter-in-law Julie, sister-in-law Janet, niece Beverley, and granddaughters Nadia, Ashley, and Holly—who all cuddled in around Dad seated in his recliner armchair.

By October, getting a picture of Dad smiling with his eyes open was tough; if he opened his eyes, he would lose the smile—and vice versa.

In 2013, smiles could still be instigated by something he enjoyed: chocolates, interaction with a staff member who was particularly attentive to him, or wearing a Santa hat on Christmas day. In 2014, when smiles were less frequent, Nadia got a smile when she did a tap dance for

Surrounded by love

Dad and told him the bird poo story they had shared years before. Dad tried a smile for Julie one morning, but would not smile for Deborah on the afternoon of the same day. By 2015, smiles were rare and looked more like a grimace. The light in Dad's eyes was long gone.

The doctor who diagnosed Dad with Alzheimer's called him garrulous. At that time, Dad was still very talkative. Nonetheless, speech was one more thing Dad gradually lost. By April 2012, conversations around him were going over his head and Dad had a tendency to separate himself from a group of visitors. Even so, he still had moments of clarity.

On a September afternoon, Janet greeted Dad saying, "Hi, Neil" and he answered, "That's my name."

Even more amazing was Dad's response to the question a nurse asked him about things he used to do. Janet mentioned that Dad was an elder at his church and the nurse asked, "Oh, what church, Neil?"

Without any hesitation Dad said, "Papakura East Presbyterian."

Clearly the words Dad had written years before in the 40-year church time capsule ran deep:

Papakura East Presbyterian Church has always been and will always be the spiritual home for my whole family . . . God through this church and the love and fellowship of His people has blessed my family and I give all praise to Him.

At the beginning of 2013, Julie observed that Dad's speech still sounded quite chirpy. But by the end of the year he had very little to say.

In a videophone chat, I watched Dad open a Christmas present and his only word was "Cheerio" when we signed off.

By the time of my Sydney visit in June 2014, Dad talked even less. Sometimes he spoke, but we weren't always sure what he was saying.

In response to a nurse asking Dad his name he said, "Philemino Asquocious."

She had no idea what he meant, but I was excited to hear this attempted reference to one of Dad's old jokes. He had signed off his 2010 letter with his comedy list of 12 names—*Neil, Charles, Alexander, Stewart, Terrence, Piccanini, Joseph, Augustus, Oscar, Philemino, Asquicious, Archiballs Muir.*

And just when we thought he could no longer talk, he would say something pertinent. When asked if he wanted a cup of tea one day, Dad replied, "That would go down well."

Another reason for lack of smiles and conversation was that Dad was often very sleepy. On my birthday in 2012, Deborah made a video of Dad saying in a barely audible voice, "Happy birthday, Angela, love, Dad."

He developed the habit of sitting with his eyes closed even if he was not sleeping. We continued to talk to him, as he seemed to hear what we were saying. But by June 2014, he was frequently not alert and was indeed nodding off.

In April 2012 it was hard to know what Dad still remembered, because he was smart enough to fudge it sometimes. He knew his immediate family but struggled to make connections after that. When Fiona and Claire visited from New Zealand, he knew who they were—although he identified them as daughters, then cousins, then correctly, as stepdaughters.

In a July 2012 visit with Janet and Ray, Dad appeared not to know their names on arrival, but said "Goodbye, Ray," as they left.

And he had correctly introduced Janet as his sister-in-law only a few days earlier. He had his good days and bad days. Dad still knew my name when I visited him in June 2014. When I read him selections from his visitor's book, he was interested and said he remembered his NZ friends—Spencer and Celia, Norma and Bill, and Ann Greene. Sadly, he hadn't remembered them on the day they visited.

In the first couple of years at Alexander Aged Care, Dad still enjoyed his photo albums and reading the newspaper. Of course, looking at the photos lasted longer than the reading, but he kept up the ritual of turning pages even after he was no longer able to read. This was evident when he had the newspaper upside down and was still turning pages.

For the most part, by this point, Dad declined to join any group activities. Though for a little while he agreed to take a turn knocking down plastic bowling pins on the patio. He much preferred the abstract painting class. This must have tapped into something deep down because as kids we appreciated his ability to draw cartoons and help mum with artwork for a Sunday school lesson.

By June 2014, Dad was barely watching TV, not even the sports he once loved. A month later, Janet tried playing tic-tac-toe (naughts and crosses) with Dad, but he could only make random marks on the page and could not write the symbols. Because Dad liked to keep his hands busy and would fiddle with the tabletop and tap it endlessly, Alexander staff gave him colored blocks to play with. When you sat next to him, Dad would take your hand and busy himself manipulating your fingers.

Physical Decline

Dad's resistance to exercise continued at Alexander Aged Care. All the same, from 2011 to 2013, family visitors insisted that he walk the Alexander hallway circuit. He would hold onto his visitor with one hand and tightly grip the handrail with the other hand. One day when Ashley was walking with Dad, she was shocked when he grabbed hold of her thigh. The handrail ran out when they reached the fire door and that was Dad's way of keeping his balance.

Dad's steps were very slow and tentative on any sloping surface. Janet and I noticed this in August 2012 when taking Dad for a drive to Balmoral Beach. Although Dad enjoyed his ice-cream, he was very nervous walking down the sloping sidewalk to the boardwalk. Greg and Julie had a similar experience in April 2012 when they took Dad out for dinner at a leagues club. The club was in walking distance—just across the street—but the sidewalk was too steep for Dad's liking.

Dad was scheduled for physical therapy sessions at Alexander, but he refused to go to the therapy room. Using the principle *if you can't beat him join him*, in August 2012 the PT brought therapy to Dad's room. She placed stand-alone bike pedals on the floor in front of him and helped him put his feet into the loops on the pedals. But it took urging from both of us to get him to rotate. He finally rotated the pedals a few times, but not enough to save his ability to walk; within a year or two he was so weak he used a wheelchair for mobility. When I saw the therapist on my June 2014 visit, she confirmed that PT was no longer beneficial for Dad.

Initially Dad used a wheelchair that belonged to Alexander Aged Care. But with a sling seat and no head support he was uncomfortable sitting in this chair for any length of time. The longer he sat in the wheelchair the more he slumped over. In 2014, Robert shared his rehabilitation engineering expertise to help us select and buy Dad a wheelchair that provided greater support and comfort.

Unaware of Milestone Events

Twenty-fourteen was a milestone year, yet Dad was unaware of all three events. In January, we sold the Whangamata beach house; in May, Dad turned 80; and in December, his brother, Stewart, succumbed to Alzheimer's disease. Even though I came to visit Dad for his birthday, he had no idea that celebration was in order. Dad didn't even look at me for the photo I took of him sitting with the array of birthday cards in front of him.

Final Stages of Disease

Dad's physical condition was also in noticeable decline. He could no longer feed himself and he was losing weight. My last entry in Dad's visitor's book on July 5, 2014:

He is in good hands here and most of all God has Dad in His Hands.

After September 2015, we stopped posting Facebook photos of Dad. Immediate family communicated Dad's health status via private texting on WhatsApp. When swallowing and choking became an issue, a speech language pathologist recommended that Dad only ingest soft food and thickened liquids. The next medical step would have been a feeding tube. But slowing down the natural process of dying would have been cruel and Dad's Advanced Care Planning directive provided that no feeding tube would be inserted.

At this stage, I began praying for God to take Dad quickly. And God was merciful. Dad never reached the point of not being able to swallow, he did not have to suffer through two weeks of starvation, and we did not have to witness it. God quickly took Dad to heaven at 9:27 a.m. on Saturday morning, May 21, 2016, one week before his 82nd birthday. Staff said they had never seen anyone go so fast. Soon after eating breakfast, Dad only suffered about one hour of respiratory distress before taking his last breath.

Saying Goodbye

We were grateful that Dad did not die alone. Deborah got there in time, but Dad died about 20 minutes before Greg arrived. I was in the room off and on via Skype all morning. One by one, family members came to say goodbye and comfort one another. As much as we knew the inevitable end of Dad's disease, we were unprepared for the emotional response of relief and grief wrapped into one.

Alexander Aged Care gave us the time we needed in Dad's room. Actually, we had more time than usual, because on the weekend there was a long wait for the doctor to come and sign the death certificate and for the funeral home to come for his body. Nobody wanted to leave Dad there alone so they waited.

Even though Dad said he wanted to be cremated, the funeral home still prepared his body for a viewing. Deborah and Julie went to see him laid out on May 24, 2016. Julie said they had very respectfully done a wonderful job and that he looked really good—even better than the last time she saw him. More importantly, Julie felt the peace of our Lord around him.

Two memorial services were held: one at Deborah and Rob's place in Sydney on May 29, 2016, and the other at Papakura East Presbyterian Church in New Zealand on July 30th. Both memorials included a slide show of Dad through the years, flowers, music, and eulogies. The Australian family memorial was more intimate with no officiating minister and invited guests only. The NZ church memorial was officiated by Reverend Michael Frost who did not know Dad and retired Reverend Andrew Bell who knew Dad very well. The service was advertised with a published obituary in the NZ Herald.

Even though Dad had not lived in New Zealand for seven years, at least 150 people remembered him well enough to attend his memorial—twice as many people as we expected. We were blown away. Auntie Joye was not in the least bit surprised, given how many lives Dad touched in his 50-plus years living in Papakura.

We also honored Dad's wishes to bury his ashes with our mother, Barbara Mary Muir, at the Papakura Old Cemetery. They had been married for 25 years when Mum died of cancer in 1980. We updated Mum's headstone by adding Dad's name with the heading "Together Again." We were confident in this, because they both believed that Jesus Christ died and rose again to save them from their sins. It all gelled when Reverend Frost preached from Psalm 23, we sang the hymn, "Surely Goodness and Mercy," and chose the epitaph, *"Dwelling in the house of the Lord forever" from Psalm 23:6.*

Celebrating my father's 81 years of life at Papakura East Presbyterian Church brought Robert and I full circle back to another celebration, 35 years earlier. In October 1981, Dad had given my hand in marriage to Robert, standing in this same sanctuary. And there we stood together again, celebrating Dad's life and his passing into eternity. ■

Epilogue

"PASS ME YOUR SHOES!" was my literal cry out to my new husband on the beach in Waikiki. I could not keep his shoes dry, but I could help him back on his feet. This honeymoon incident was a picture of the stumbles and falls we experienced early in our marriage for failing to follow in God's steps. Yet just as God allowed Jacob to receive the blessing of his father Isaac despite his deception, God blessed our marriage despite our initial dishonesty. And just as Jacob suffered when his father-in-law gave Leah as his wife instead of Rachel, we suffered as victims of betrayal, theft, fraud, and embezzlement.

Although God's correction achieved His purpose of bringing us to repentance, we each walked in our own shoes at a different pace. My conviction and confession quickly flowed from studying God's Word while Robert's came after struggling for survival in his marriage, business, and health. Robert finally admitted that his best efforts would never be enough to please either God or me—he surrendered to God and trusted Him for salvation, wisdom, and strength.

Once we were both back on track with a desire to please God, we got back in step with one another. Marriage counseling was the key to our improved communication, learning more about walking in Love and as children of Light:

> And walk in love, just as Christ also loved]you and gave Himself up for us, an offering and a sacrifice to God . . .
> for you were formerly darkness, but now you are Light in the Lord; walk as children of Light (for the fruit of the Light consists in all goodness and righteousness and truth), trying to learn what is pleasing to the Lord.
> ∞ Ephesians 5:2, 8-10

As we began trying to learn what is pleasing to the Lord, we were better equipped to serve God in Christian ministry—not perfect, of course— but growing. As with any Christian in spiritual warfare, our trials continued. But we persevered:

> But that's not all! Even in times of trouble we have a joyful confidence, knowing that our pressures will develop in us patient endurance. And patient endurance will refine our character, and proven character leads us back to hope. ∞ Romans 5:3-4, TPT

Our marriage story continues beyond the pages of this book until death do us part. We pray that our story might bring hope to you in your own journey, whether you're being thrashed by turbulent waves, or peacefully walking the tranquil shore. God is always beside you, talking to you, and leading you while holding both your right hand and your shoes. ■

Preview of Book III

ALWAYS AN ADVOCATE:
A Couple with Dwarfism
Fight for Independence and Respect

Chapter 4
Breaking the Six-Inch Reach Barrier

The ATM Problem

The bank was closed on the weekend, we needed cash, and at 54 inches the ATM was out of Robert's reach. Not deterred by a six-inch reach barrier, he backed up our Honda wagon to the ATM, opened the hatchback and stood on the bumper. Mission accomplished, or so he thought. A police officer stopped him from leaving the scene after witnessing his suspicious behavior.

After seeing that Robert hadn't emptied all of the ATM cash into the trunk, the officer let him off with a warning, "Don't do this again."

So, what were little people supposed to do to gain access to ATMs? The federal Access Board—responsible for setting accessibility standards under the Americans with Disabilities Act of 1990 (ADA)—seemed like a good place to start. Robert and I were among the 700 LPA members and associates who responded to the Access Board's call for public comments on the height of ATMs; Nancy Mayeux, a Florida parent of two children with dwarfism, led the LPA letter-writing campaign asking for ATMs to be lowered six inches, from 54 to 48 inches.

LPA's hopes for equal access under the ADA were dashed on July 15, 1993. The powerful banking industry persuaded the Access Board to allow operable parts on ATMs to remain out of reach at 54 inches. The board cited the need for further research on the reach range of little people and the implications for taller people. The blow was devastating. How would we ever achieve independence if the Access Board was more willing to accommodate the banking industry than the people who use their equipment?

One year later, LPA learned that a better place to start was the ICC/ ANSI (International Code Council/American National Standards Institute) A117.1 Committee on Accessible and Usable Buildings and Facilities (ANSI Access Committee). LPA had never heard of it until John Salmen—an architect member representing the American Hotel and Lodging Association—approached LPA President Ruth Ricker in July 1994. John explained that the ANSI Access Committee produced the equivalent of a model building code used to make public buildings and facilities accessible to people with disabilities. John realized that the 700 letters from LPA members hadn't achieved the desired result; he encouraged LPA not to give up. He revealed that the ANSI Access Committee was ready to hear about the access needs of little people and nudged LPA to apply for membership in the category designated for users requiring accessibility.

President Ruth accepted John's advice that the beginning of the ANSI Access Code three-year revision cycle was the perfect time for LPA to submit proposed changes. Thus, she obtained LPA Board approval to apply for membership. Now all Ruth needed was to appoint a delegate to represent LPA at the meetings. She offered me this assignment given my background as an attorney and advocate. I didn't doubt my qualifications, but I did question the volunteer assignment given the enormity of the charge. The six-inch reach barrier applied not only to ATMs, but also to bathrooms, elevator buttons, public telephones, pay-at-the pump fuel dispensers, door and window handles, and laundry and kitchen appliances—everything open to the public activated with a push, pull or turn.

Robert forewarned me about the difficulty of the task, but LPA's recent advocacy defeat on the height of ATMs was fresh on my mind. He remembered the telephone industry's successful opposition to lowering the height of public pay phones when he worked for the federal Access Board as a communications engineer in 1981.

But ringing in my ears was the question of a teenage little person in one of my LPA advocacy workshops, "Who is going to do something about the height of ATMs?"

At the time, I had no answer for Ginny.

Now I had no answer for President Ruth when she said, "If you don't do it, Angela, who will?"◆

Acknowledgments

Although this is not an awards ceremony where I will be played off the stage after my allotted time, there is the same risk of overlooking the unforgettable person who contributed to the production and success of this book. So, to that unnamed person, I say thank you.

To those named below I am eternally grateful for your encouragement, enduring support, and expertise through the many years it has taken to produce this book.

Editor: Vicki Prather,
   pratherink.wordpress.com/mrs-p-edits/
Publisher: B New Creations ~ Betty Shoopman
Front Cover Artist: Betty Shoopman
Author/Coach: Ava Pennington, avapennington.com
   Feedback on early draft manuscript: Joan Ablon,
   Angie and Lee Fielder, Beverley Heslop, Julie
   Muir, Lorrie Reckamp, Robert Van Etten, and
   Carol Wintercorn
Feedback on published manuscript: Sherri Bryan,
Dianne Callender, Angie and Lee Fielder, Darrell Pace,
Carol Snyder, Diane Tomasik, Robert Van Etten, and
Carol Wintercorn
Feedback on individual chapter drafts: Deborah
Coote, Janet Gedge, Juliette Glasow, Beverley Heslop,
and Greg Muir
Book Launch Team members
Back cover photo: Susan Sprayberry
Website—angelamuirvanetten.com:
   —Brenda Bell, BCP Data Services Inc.

About the Author

As a dual citizen of New Zealand and the United States, **Angela Muir Van Etten** qualified as a lawyer in both countries and served as national president of both Little People organizations. At three-feet-four-inches, Angela has twice been awarded LPA's highest honor, the Kitchens Meritorious Service Award. Angela and her husband married in 1981 and currently live in Stuart, Florida, where she serves as church clerk and teaches in AWANA, adult Sunday school, and Vacation Bible School.

Angela has been a legal writer and editor of law books for Thomson Reuters, a staff writer for the Christian Law Association, and a disability advocate for the Coalition for Independent Living Options. Her articles on dwarfism advocacy have published in the LPA magazine, LPA Today, and online in the HuffPost blog. You can read more of Angela's writing at her website, angelamuirvanetten.com.

Angela has media and public speaking experience in local, regional, national, and international markets. TV icons such as Phil Donahue, Sally Jessy Raphael, and John Stossel all interviewed Angela during her mission to ban dwarf tossing as barroom entertainment.

Notes

Chapter 1 My Heart Beat Faster

[1] Associated Press, Christopher Connell, "Little People's President Has Conservative Views Tested," February 5, 1981.
Laura Kierman, "Job Freeze by Reagan is Upheld," *The Washington Post*, (February 26, 1981).
John Hicks, "Left out in cold, he chips at ice on federal hiring," *Sentinel Star*, (Orlando, FL), March 1, 1981.

[2] "Larsen Syndrome," LPA Medical Resource Center, Dwarfism Types and Diagnoses, accessed April 22, 2019), https://www.lpaonline.org/medical-resource-center.

[3] University of Texas v. Camenisch, 451 U.S. 390 (1981).

Chapter 2, Whirlwind Romance

[1] Cox News Service (Washington, DC), Bud Newman, "Long Worthwhile Wait: Job Finally Comes Through for Hardship Case," *The Post*, April 1, 1981.
John Hicks, "It's Like Being Rescued from a Sinking Ship," *The Sentinel Star*, (Orlando, FL) April 2, 1981.
United Press International (Winter Park), "Dwarf Wins Long Battle for Federal Job," *Sarasota Herald Tribune*, April 3, 1981.

[2] In 1981 the Committee was known as "the President's Committee on Employment of the Handicapped."

[3] Ed Lang, "Prince Bob to wed Lady Angela," LPA *Today*, September 1981, 4.

Chapter 3, A Cord of Three Strands

[1] *The Evening Post*, (Wellington, NZ), October 20, 1981, 32.

[2] "A little love has gone a long, long way . . .," *Sentinel Star*, (Orlando, FL), December 1, 1981.

[3] Amanda Samuel, "Just two people in love, beginning a new life," *New Zealand Woman's Weekly*, November 23, 1981, 12.

[4] John Hicks, "Two Little People take the Big Step," *Sentinel Star*, (Orlando, FL), December 1, 1981.

Chapter 6, Fundraising and Principle

[1] "Benjamin Franklin Quotes About Integrity," AZ Quotes, accessed May 20, 2020, https://www.azquotes.com/author/5123-Benjamin_Franklin/tag/integrity.

[2] John Keats, AZQuotes.com, (Wind and Fly LTD, 2020), accessed May 20, 2020, https://www.azquotes.com/quote/1043909.

Chapter 7, Cleveland Changes

[1] William Blake Quotes, BrainyQuote.com, BrainyMedia Inc, 2020, accessed May 18, 2020, https://www.brainyquote.com/quotes/william_blake_101447.

[2] Jonathon Berlin and Kori Rumore, "Chicago's coldest recorded temperatures," Chicago Tribune, pub. January 30, 2020: 7:57 a.m., https://www.chicagotribune.com/weather/ct-met-viz-chicago-record-coldest-days-htmlstory.html.

Chapter 8, New York Beginnings
[1] Eric Gunn, "The tall problems of little people," *Democrat and Chronicle*, (Rochester, NY edition), June 2, 1985.

Chapter 9, Home at Last
1 Dianne Carraway, "Little People group wants to show size isn't everything," *Rochester Times Union*, (Rochester, NY), May 12, 1987.

[2] Angela Muir Van Etten, *Dwarfs Don't Live in Doll Houses*, (Adaptive Living, 1988).

[3] Van Etten, *Jeder Mensch: Wird Klein Geboren Autobiographieeiner Kleinwuchsigen*, trans. Helga Kramer, (Recklinghausen: Georg Bitter Verlag KG, 1992).

Chapter 10, Season of Travel
[1] Robert presented his fellowship report in New Orleans at the 1989 June RESNA Conference and in Washington, DC, at the World Rehabilitation Conference on Technology.

[2] Abby Karp, "Little People's Biggest Problem: Small Minds," *The Baltimore Sun*, July 3, 1989. Shirley Marlow, "In No Small Feat, She Finds True Stature as a Writer," *Los Angeles Times*, July 4, 1989.

Chapter 11, Prayer and Protection
[1] Gary Smalley and John Trent, *Love is a Decision*, (Word Publishing, 1989).

[2] Angela Muir Van Etten, ed., *Americans with Disabilities: Practice and Compliance Manual*, Lawyers Cooperative Publishing, a division of Thomson Legal Publishing, Inc. Copyright © 1992.
The publication also covered disability civil rights laws, such as: The Air Carrier Access Act of 1986, the Communications Act of 1934, the Fair Housing Amendments Act of 1988, the Individuals with Disabilities Education Act of 1975, the Rehabilitation Act of 1973, and the Voting Accessibility for the Elderly and Handicapped Act of 1984.

[3] Robert A. Weisgerber, "Problem Solving from a Different Perspective," in *The Challenged Scientists: Disabilities and the Triumph of Excellence*, (Preager, New York, 1991), 157-162.

[4] Robert was a member of the following Committees:
- Technical Access Advisory Committee, New York State Advocates Office for the Disabled (1990-1991)
- New York State Board of Regents Select Committee on Disability (1991-1992)
- New York State Technology Related Assistance for Individuals with Disabilities Advisory Board (1991-1993)
- The RESNA Service Delivery Special Interest Committee (1990 1991)
- The American Association for Advancement in Science Advisory Board for Disabled Engineers in College (1991-1997)

Chapter 12, Seeing the Light of Day

1   The CCS acronym is no longer spelled out—Crippled Children's Society—because the word "crippled" is outdated and offensive. Because the organization was so well known by its acronym, the organization name was simply changed to CCS. Sometime later, the name was expanded to CCS Disability Action. CCS Disability Action, accessed January 10, 2020, https://ccsdisabilityaction.org.nz.

Chapter 14, What a Difference Ten Years Makes

1   Kathleen Driscoll, "10 years of helping the disabled to adapt," *Times-Union*, (Rochester, New York), March 30, 1995.

2   Robert was a board member of the Rochester Rehabilitation Center from 1995-1997.

3   *The Americans with Disabilities: Practice and Compliance Manual* spawned a legal textbook called *Americans with Disabilities: Analysis and Implications* published with me as the named author (New York: Lawyers Cooperative Publishing, 1993).

4   Thomson Legal Publishing (TLP) purchased LCP in 1989. However, when TLP purchased LCP's competitor, West Publishing in 1996 the corporate headquarters moved to Eagan, Minnesota. The closure of the Rochester printing plant cost 650 jobs.

5   Bill and Lynne Hybels, *Fit to be Tied: Making Marriage Last a Lifetime*, (Grand Rapids: Zondervan 1991).

6   Dr. John Gray, *Men are from Mars, Women are from Venus*, (Harper Collins, 1993).

Chapter 17, Putting Down Roots

1   Issues range from the freedom of students and employees to pray, read their Bibles, or wear Christian jewelry or messages on their clothing to censorship of street preachers and musicians; and from tax and zoning problems to public officials' rights; and local governments' right to pray and post the Ten Commandments.

Chapter 18, Returning to Familiar Territory

1   He exhibited the Ergo Chair from 2000 through 2018 at LPA conferences in Minneapolis, Toronto, Salt Lake City, Boston, San Francisco, Orlando, Milwaukee, Seattle, Detroit, Brooklyn, Nashville, Anaheim, Dallas, San Diego, and Denver.

2   "The fortress city of 'Minas Tirith' and 'Helm's Deep' at Dry Creek Quarry on Western Hutt Road at the bottom of Haywards Hill in Wellington," *Movie Locations*, January 10, 2020, https://www.movie-locations.com/movies/l/Lord-Of-The-Rings-The-Two-Towers.php.

3   A NZ species of clam with a large asymmetrical shell with the hinge at one side.

4   Articles were published in CLA's monthly newsletters, books, and seminar materials; the National Liberty Journal, and the Church Business Magazine. I relished the diverse subject matter, including the worldwide persecution of Christians; the Pledge of Allegiance; separation of church and state; teaching creation science in public schools; adoption; the National Day of Prayer; a Roe v. Wade anniversary; crisis pregnancy ministries; witnessing in public places; a religious conviction against working on Sundays; and the tax-exemption of churches.

Chapter 19, Everything Broke Loose

[1] Dan Rather, "Hurricane Lili / Gulf Coast / Louisiana / Frank Interview," #711414 CBS Evening News for Wednesday, Oct 02, 2002, The Vanderbilt Television News Archive, https://tvnews.vanderbilt.edu/broadcasts/711414

[2] "Abraham Lincoln's Thanksgiving Proclamation," *Lincoln and Thanksgiving*, National Park Service, Last updated January 30, 2016, https://home.nps.gov/liho/learn/historyculture/lincoln-and-thanksgiving.htm.

[3] Robert's friendship with Deborah Dagit, a former chief diversity officer at Merck's Whitehouse Station, New Jersey headquarters, opened the door for Entry Point!'s introduction to Merck.

Chapter 21, Ministry and Hospitality

[1] Enami, Etsuko, Little People, Photo Essay, (Yoshihiro Nishiyama, 2005).

[2] Robert and I were kissing in front of the Christmas tree, relaxing in the lounge, and riding with family in the boat named *Cork It*. Dwarfism issues were illustrated with contrasting photos of me in our accessible kitchen beside one of me in a relative's inaccessible kitchen. Action photos included one of Robert pumping gas, and another with sparks flying as he sharpened the blade of a spade.

[3] Approved Workers Are Not Ashamed (AWANA), (2 Timothy 2:15 ESV), accessed January 10, 2020, http://awana.org/ .

[4] Angel Tree® is a program of Prison Fellowship®, accessed January 10, 2020, https://www.prisonfellowship.org/about/angel-tree/.

[5] "Paul Harvey's Easter Story: Jesus and the Cage," *Paul Harvey*, ABC RADIO, Apr 9, 2004, https://reasonsforhopejesus.com/thebirdcage/.

Chapter 22, A Dose of Humility

[1] Kimberly Amadeo, "Hurricane Katrina Facts, Damage, and Costs," Updated June 25, 2019, http://useconomy.about.com/od/grossdomesticproduct/f/katrina damage.htm.
Allison Plyer, "Facts for Features: Katrina Impact," The Data Center, pub. August 26, 2016, https://www.datacenterresearch.org/data-resources/katrina/facts-for-impact/.

[2] From August to December 2005, Southern Baptists prepared and served more than 13 million meals. Disaster relief units from 41 state or regional conventions responded with 9,000 volunteers who cooked, cleaned out mud, cut and removed downed trees, laundered clothes and provided shower services. Southern Baptists also gave or pledged more than $21 million to meet immediate survival needs of hurricane victims. "2005 IN REVIEW: Hurricane Katrina, Asian tsunami lead list of top stories of the year," *Baptist Press*, December 29, 2005, http://www.bpnews.net/bpnews.asp?ID=22369.
LPA offered a hardship membership to those unable to pay their dues because of time off work, job loss, home repairs or relocation expenses. Good Neighbor and Disaster Funds were set up for members needing financial assistance in District 8 (Louisiana and Texas) and District 13 (Alabama and Mississippi). Angela Van Etten, Vice President of Membership Report, *LPA Today*, Winter Issue 2005.

[3] Matt Hannafin, "Hurricane Wilma Flattens Cozumel, Sweeps Florida, Impacting Caribbean Cruise Routes," October 26, 2005, https://www.frommers.com/tips/cruise/hurricane-wilma-flattens-cozumel-sweeps-florida-impacting-caribbean-cruise-routes; Suzanne Wentley, "Experts surprised by Wilma's power," accessed October 25, 2005.

[4] Wentley, "Wilma again a Category 3 as it moves offshore," accessed October 24, 2005, http://www.tcpalm.com/tcp/hurricane_news/article/0,2544,TCP_1239_4181965,00.html.

[5] Wentley, "Experts surprised by Wilma's power," accessed October 24, 2005, http://www.tcpalm.com/tcp/hurricane_news/article/0,2544,TCP_1239_4184085,00.html. "Hurricanes and Tropical Storms - Annual 2005," National Oceanic and Atmospheric Administration, National Centers for Environmental Information, accessed April 25, 2019, https://www.ncdc.noaa.gov/sotc/tropical-cyclones/200513.

[6] Associated Press, Melissa Trujillo, "President Bush visits Wilma victims, pledges return to normal," accessed October 27, 2005, http://www.tcpalm.com/tcp/wptv/article/0,2547,TCP_1213_4192553,00.html.

[7] Associated Press, (New Mexican), Trujillo, "Hurricane Wilma: Lights back on for many in Florida," accessed October 29, 2005, http://www.freenewmexican.com/news/34363.html.

[8] Jim Turner, "Stuart Causeway reopens; residential damage in Martin reaches $50 million," accessed October 28, 2005, http://www.tcpalm.com/tcp/local_news/article/0,2545,TCP_16736_4192007,00.html

Chapter 23, Aortic Valve Replacement

[1] "Top Thoracic and Cardiac Surgeons," *U.S. News and World Report*, accessed October 13, 2012, http://health.usnews.com/top-doctors/directory/best-cardiac-thoracic-surgeons.

[2] CarePages is no longer available, but a similar service is provided at CaringBridge, accessed January 10, 2020, https://www.caringbridge.org/.

[3] Beth Moore. *Breaking Free*, Week 1: "Untying the Cords of the Yoke", Day 5: "The Reign of Christ," (Lifeway Press. 1999: updated 2009), 28.

[4] Moore, Week 3: "Removing the Obstacles," Day 4: "The Obstacle of Prayerlessness," 71.

ALWAYS AN ADVOCATE: Chapter 4, Breaking the Six-Inch Reach Barrier

[1] "Rule-making History," United States Access Board, accessed April 25, 2019, https://www.access-board.gov/guidelines-and-standards/buildings-and-sites/about-the-ada-standards/background/proposed-ada-and-aba-accessibility-guidelines/background.

[2] The ANSI Access Code becomes enforceable law when adopted by state and local governments. Many of its provisions even form the basis for the federal access code known as the ADAAG which becomes enforceable law when adopted by federal government agencies.